RECOLLECTIONS OF A
LONG LIFE · 1829-1915

Isaac Stephenson

RECOLLECTIONS OF A LONG LIFE · 1829-1915

BY

ISAAC STEPHENSON

CHICAGO
PRIVATELY PRINTED
1915

PREFACE

IN undertaking to set down, so that others may read, the recollections of my own personal experiences during three-quarters of a century or more, it is not my purpose to trespass upon the field either of the historian or of the commentator by attempting to interpret the events which came directly or indirectly under my observation.

Nor is it my purpose to point a moral. What I have written is no more than a concise narrative of what befell me, of the difficulties I encountered, the disappointments I suffered and the triumphs I achieved, the fortunes and misfortunes that were dealt out to me by my controlling destiny.

There are few men living who have had so varied, certainly so long, a career as I. It is a far cry from the agitation over the northeastern boundary controversy in 1839 to the vicissitudes of latter-day politics in 1915. Many things have happened within that space of time. The greater portion of the country has been transformed from a wilderness into a cultivated and settled area. Railroads have intersected it; cities have been built; and its vitality has awakened to the pulsations of a highly organized commercial life.

In that epoch of progress I moved as an individual with the flowing stream, but I no less than the others have seen something of the changes that have been wrought, the decay of old customs and the growth of new, the succession of problems from meeting the rigors of the wilderness to the adjustment of social and economic relations in the complex civilization of to-day. If this viewpoint from a lengthy perspective will enable anyone who may read to measure with greater accuracy of vision the advantages and disadvantages of the shifting present, I shall count what I have written as of some value.

The migration of the lumbermen of the Maine and New Brunswick forests — in the early part of the last century the greatest center of the industry in the world — is one of the interesting phases of the pioneer period of American history. They blazed a way with restless energy into the timbered wilderness of Pennsylvania, of Wisconsin and Michigan, of Minnesota, of the mountain region of the far West and finally of the Pacific coast. From ocean to ocean the tide has moved within the span of my own lifetime.

A part of that course it was my lot to travel. I journeyed from Maine to Boston by sea, from Boston to Albany by train, from Albany to Buffalo by canal-boat and thence over the Great Lakes, the main thoroughfare from the expanding West, to Milwaukee before the railroads extended beyond Buffalo and many of the great cities of the country were more than a name. Of the early settlements along Green Bay and the northern peninsula of Michigan struggling for foothold on the verge of what seemed to be almost illimitable forests I have watched the growth, and the wilderness I have seen melt away before the encroaching stretch of farms.

My experiences were, in large measure, the experiences of those who set the pace of achievement under these conditions. I worked with them exploring the forests, in the logging camps, on the rivers and at the mills, and sailed with them on Lake Michigan as seaman, mate, and master.

Favored by circumstance, I covered wider fields than most of them. From the time I fell under the eye of my mother's cousin, Christopher Murray, at Murray Castle, Spring Hill, New Brunswick, when I was four years old, it was my good fortune to attract the attention and enjoy the confidence of many men. I came to the West as a member of the household of Jefferson Sinclair, the greatest practical lumberman of his time; was associated in business with William B. Ogden, at one time mayor of Chicago, also one of the towering figures of his day; and numbered among my friends Samuel J. Tilden and a host of other men of large affairs — lawyers, railroad builders, bankers, manufacturers — who set the seal of their energy upon the broadening destiny of the country,—pioneers, no less, of their kind.

By reason, no doubt, of the knowledge I had gained of conditions in northern Wisconsin and Michigan and the training I had received at the hands of Mr. Sinclair, a score of offers of employment were made to me by men who desired me to take charge of lumbering, mining, land, and railroad-building enterprises. It is possible, therefore, that some idea of the difficulties these men encountered and the ordeals through which they passed may be gathered from this narrative, although it is a purely personal one, my own story told in my own way.

Whether a comparison of the present manner of living with that which prevailed in those early days would point the way to reforms I doubt much. Changing standards offer a cloak for lapses from hard-and-fast rules of conduct, and the judgments of one generation are held not to apply in another. None the less the necessity which confronted these hewers of wood and drawers of water was a wholesome stimulant. The long days of hard work bred sturdy, if not facile, character — a lesson which no age is too advanced in wisdom to learn.

In this time of social and economic readjustment it might be well to remember that their achievement was due to industry and thrift and that the opportunity which looms large in retrospect was less apparent in their immediate environment than that which the future now seems to hold.

Too often, as I see it, the background of toil and struggle is left to hazy outline while the results of their labors are blazoned forth in vivid colors. Accordingly is the measure of their compensation exaggerated and the extent of their effort minimized. What allurement did the prospect of an isolated wilderness possess for those who turned their faces westward? The prairies stretched for almost countless miles to regions unmapped and unexplored. The pine forests had no bounds. With such abundance mere possession availed nothing. The only wealth to be obtained was wrested from them by grinding labor; and these men labored from dawn to twilight, valorous, undaunted, and unafraid.

I have seen this period of construction pass and the chief function of government change, for the moment at least, from the stimulation to the regulation of effort. In the cycle of progress and growth of a country so blessed with abundance as ours, this, no doubt, is necessary. Adroitness has in too many cases been made to serve the purposes of toil. But in the light of the philosophy of my own experience I should choose my steps carefully lest I put upon honest effort an unnecessary burden or take from it its just reward. Progressivism and reform are a resonant shibboleth. I should demand from those who cry it other credentials than a loud voice.

Whether, when viewed from the perspective of a hundred years hence, it will be observed that greater progress was made in the earlier years of the nineteenth century than in the earlier years of the twentieth, I shall not presume to predict. I only hope that progress has been made, is being made, and will continue to be made without let or hindrance and that the problems of life will be met and solved as they arise, to the happiness and contentment of human kind. Isaac Stephenson

LIST OF ILLUSTRATIONS

CONTENTS

CHAPTER I

CHAPTER II

CHAPTER III

11

CHAPTER IV

CHAPTER V

CHAPTER VI

CHAPTER VII

CHAPTER VIII

CHAPTER IX

CHAPTER X

CHAPTER XI

CHAPTER XII

CHAPTER XIII

CHAPTER XIV

CHAPTER XV

CONTENTS 15

CHAPTER XX

CHAPTER XXI

RECOLLECTIONS OF A LONG LIFE · 1829-1915

CHAPTER I

My great-grandfather, Andrew Stephenson, emigrates from Scotland to Ireland and becomes owner of farm and flax-mill in Raphoe, Donegal County — Robert Stephenson, my grandfather, in charge of property — The Ulster blood — My father, Isaac Stephenson, born in 1790 — Difficulties in Ireland — Father sails in 1809 for America — Life in New Brunswick — Takes charge of Loyalist estates — Colonel Allen — The Murrays and Spring Hill — Colonel Wilmot — Father marries Elizabeth Watson — Colonel Miles and my birth-place, Maugerville — Residence at Hartland, Nevers estate, and Greenfield.

THE fortunes of my forbears, like the family chronicles of many of the Scotch-Irish whose names appear frequently in American annals, follow in general outline, but with divergent detail, the history of the Scotch emigration to Ulster and the subsequent exodus from that province to America.

Family tradition throws little light on the estate of the Stephensons prior to the time of my great-grandfather, Andrew Stephenson. What his career was can only be dimly surmised from the general drift of large affairs in Ulster during the period following the revolution. On the subject of his personal activities no records survive and tradition is almost blank. Like so many others who have sought their fortunes in far places, he came from the lowlands of Scotland, where the name Stephenson flourished. Here also, it is probable, originated the family to which George Stephenson, the distinguished engineer and inventor, and his son Robert, also an engineer, belonged. The story has been told from one generation to another, at least in my own branch of this seemingly numerous clan, that Andrew Stephenson, my great-grandfather, and George Stephenson, the engineer, came of the same stock.[1]

Andrew Stephenson went to Ireland some time during the first half of the eighteenth century. In this venture, probably, he merely followed the example of many of his hardier neighbors who were ready to abandon the land of their birth, where increasing numbers made the scramble for a competency difficult, for the less restricted territory wrested from the native Irish. Others of the name had gone before him. It appears in Pynnar's survey of the province of Ulster and in various other records of the affairs of that settlement. But there is nothing to indicate that my great-grandfather did not go entirely upon his own initiative. The tradition of the family is that he was given lands in Donegal, possibly some of the territory forfeited by an absentee landlord of the earlier settlement or an unfortunate proprietor attainted of treason.

In any event he settled in Raphoe, not far from the city of Strabane, and became the owner of a farm and a flax-mill. The farm, called Culladerry, evidently a property of some proportions, lay in the heart of the flax region

---

[1] George Stephenson, who built the first passenger railroad from Liverpool to Manchester, and the first locomotive, the Rocket, used on the line, was born in the village of Wylam, eight miles west of Newcastle-on-Tyne. "A tradition is, indeed, preserved in the family that old Robert Stephenson's father (George Stephenson's great-grandfather) and mother came across the border from Scotland on the loss of considerable property there." Smiles' *Life of George Stephenson;* John Murray: London, 1857.

which, as a later traveler has observed, may be perceived
at some distance in the late summer when the fields are
in blossom "from the abominable odor of that fibrous
plant." The deed to the property, corresponding to our
present-day warranty deed, confirmed title to the possession "as long as the grass grows and the water runs."
At Culladerry also was the flax-mill, probably what was
known as a scutching-mill, one of the small units that
went to make up the flourishing linen industry of the
period. The product of this establishment was disposed
of at Strabane, to which my elders referred oftentimes,
when I was a child in New Brunswick, as "oor market
toon."

In this environment Andrew Stephenson seems to have
prospered and was considered, as fortunes were measured
at the time, a well-to-do, if not wealthy, man. He survived at least, the vicissitudes to which the linen and
other industries were subjected by adverse legislation,
export taxes and the setbacks of an occasional bad year,
which impelled thousands of weavers and other linen-
workers to emigrate to the colonies in America. He did
not suffer much, if at all, from religious disturbances or
business reverses during a rather difficult period and,
whatever his lot, remained at Culladerry, reared a family,
and in the fullness of his time died and was buried where
he had lived and labored.

My grandfather, Robert Stephenson, succeeded to
possession of the property. Although he was born more
than a century and a half ago, in 1753, and was in the
flower of early manhood at the time of the American Revolution, he appears to me in a much more personal light than
his predecessors. He came to New Brunswick after my
father had pointed the way, and died, when more than

eighty years of age, in the stone house where he had lived, a few miles from the city of Fredericton, on the St. John River, when I was a small boy. Here also my grandmother died at about the age of ninety.

Robert Stephenson was a soft-spoken, mild-mannered man, possessing, however, the typical Ulster characteristic of an indomitable will, which, transmitted to succeeding generations, accounts in large measure, I have no doubt, for the perseverance that has brought success to many of Scotch-Irish descent in the United States. His decision of character is exemplified in two incidents of his career which stand out rather prominently from the body of domestic tradition centering upon him.

One of the prominent residents of the neighborhood of Culladerry was a Judge Lindsley, a man of quite as much determination as my grandfather. The Lindsley family was also of Scotch origin and occupied a conspicuous position socially and commercially in the affairs of the county. In the rôle of suitor to his daughter Margaret,— who was almost a giantess in strength and physique,— my grandfather did not appear in a favorable light in the sight of Judge Lindsley, and to gain his end was obliged to resort to the old method of elopement. From the time of her marriage my grandmother never saw her father; and he, dogged to the end, did not once mention her name, it was said, after she had deserted the parental roof. The fact of her existence was called to his attention when he was on his death bed, but her name did not appear among the beneficiaries under his will.

Members of the Lindsley family also sought their fortunes in America. My grandmother's brother owned a farm within the present limits of the city of Philadelphia, where he and two men whom he employed were killed by

Indians. More than sixty years ago we contemplated engaging Daniel Webster as counsel and having a search made of the records which might disclose our interest in the property as heirs through my grandmother, but because of the serious obstacles in the way of establishing the claim and the time that had elapsed since the death of my great-uncle we abandoned the project.

In later years my grandfather was afflicted with rheumatism and was compelled to use crutches, but this physical disability apparently did not result in any diminution of his indomitable spirit. It flared forth on one occasion when the dam by which the water power for the flax-mill was generated was in need of repairs. The task was undertaken by some of his sons and employees while he stood by on his crutches watching the progress of the work. The weather was cold. There was snow on the ground and the men were reluctant to go into the icy water. Their attempts to evade the ordeal stirred his Ulster blood and at length, throwing aside all precaution and his crutches as well, he plunged into the chilly stream himself. Instead of paying for his rashness with more acute rheumatic pains he recovered entirely from his ailment, as a result of his bath, so the story is told, and was able to dispense with the crutches for the remainder of his days.

My father, Isaac Stephenson, was the fifth of seventeen children, fifteen of whom eventually came to America in accordance with the plans he had in large measure made for them. At the time of his birth in 1790 conditions in Ireland were none too good. He grew up in an environment of stress and struggle to make ends meet. Although the Stephensons were in much better position financially than most of their neighbors in the flax region, a family of such proportions undoubtedly presented economic problems which even the resources of a large farm and flax mill could not obviate altogether. In Raphoe and Donegal increasing restrictions upon the linen trade had put a blight upon the flax industry. The country was impoverished and held no promise for the young man who looked to the future for opportunities for advancement.

The exodus from the north of Ireland, which had drained the country of many thousands of its best men and women during the latter part of the eighteenth century, was still in progress when my father was a boy, and he was but one of many who followed in its wake in the first years of the nineteenth century. From the earlier colonists came reports of prosperity and success in the New World. The big timber-ships from Maine and New Brunswick ports which put into Londonderry, not far from Raphoe, laden with masts and spars and hewn logs of a size unknown in the sparse forests of Ireland, bore tangible evidence of the wealth overseas and not only excited the imagination of the people but afforded the means of flight from the trying conditions surrounding them.

To add to the difficulties of the Stephenson family, reverses overtook my grandfather through the escapades of one of his sons who had set out for Scotland to buy horses. In this dilemma my father found inspiration in the stories of opportunity in America, which were doubtless borne from Londonderry down the valley of the Foyle, and he decided to join the stream of travelers who went there to seek their fortunes.

He set sail in 1809, when he was nineteen years old, from Londonderry where, doubtless, many of the progenitors of the Scotch-Irish and Irish families now in the United States and Canada also embarked. How momentous these voyages must have seemed to them as they watched the shores of the land they knew recede, may be left to imagination. Conditions on board the timber ships, although they were more commodious than most sailing vessels, were none too luxurious. Their destination was from six to ten weeks away, with the threat of storm and rough weather constantly hovering over them. These rigors, however, did not check the flow of emigration.

My father landed at the port of St. John, New Brunswick, then one of the busiest cities on the western continent, with a population of approximately thirty-five hundred. Thence he went up the St. John River to Fredericton, where the land of opportunity lay. Having probably scant resources except his own energy, and following the example of those about him, he secured employment at once, lumbering on the Oromocto River several miles below the town.

Life along the St. John was still largely of the mold in which it was cast when the land bordering upon it was parceled out in large tracts to early colonists or Loyalist refugees from the states. These families carried with them the aristocratic traditions of the older countries, and those who considered themselves as belonging to this social category sought to reproduce the manner of living which prevailed in the British Isles. Even in my own day a justice of the peace, or squire, was a dignitary of much consequence, and the Loyalist grantees — who were referred to colloquially as Bluenoses — maintained their elevated positions with unrelaxing vigilance. In many instances they erected large houses which were called — at least by us children — castles, and left the management of their estates, some of them consisting of thousands of acres, to an overseer, if they were fortunate enough to find one capable of performing that function.

This condition, as it happened, had an important bearing upon my father's career in more ways than one. Being a man of great industry and obviously of more than ordinary capacity, he was sought out by the Loyalist grantees and men of large affairs to take charge of their properties until he achieved an independent position. While so engaged he met and married a member of one of the most distinguished families of the period, which, divided in its allegiance, rendered almost as conspicuous service in the cause of the American Revolution as it did in the cause of the Crown.

After lumbering for two or three years on the Oromocto, where masts were being cut for the Royal Navy, my father was engaged by Colonel Isaac Allen to manage his estate on the St. John River, six miles above Fredericton. This property covered the territory formerly occupied by the old Indian village of Aukpaque and included within its limits Savage Island and Sugar Island. It was also the site of an old French mission in the vicinity of which had been an Acadian settlement, some of the residents of which still lingered when my father assumed direction of affairs. Although little trouble was encountered with the Indians, some of whom also remained in the neighborhood, my father narrowly escaped death at the hands of one of them. While he was hoeing corn on Savage Island a member of the tribe which had once camped there, fired with rum, threw a tomahawk at him. Fortunately the weapon missed its mark and before the Indian could do greater harm my father laid his head open with the hoe, all but killing him. I had occasion to remember this incident because some years afterward my brother nearly severed two of my fingers with the same tomahawk, and I have borne the scar left by the wound ever since.

Adjoining the Allen estate and separated from it by a small stream was Spring Hill, the estate of the Murray family, one of the most important points in the lumbering industry on the St. John River. It lay at the head of tidewater, where the small rafts, in which form timber and logs were transported from the upper river below Grand Falls, were made up into larger rafts to be dropped down to the city of St. John with the tide. As a child I saw thousands of these rafts at Spring Hill, covering in unbroken mass acres of the surface of the river.

Of the four brothers of the Murray family, who resided in New York at the opening of the Revolutionary War, two, Christopher and Robert, cast their lot with the colonists, while the others, William and John, remained loyal to the Crown. As a penalty for their Toryism the latter, with the other Loyalists, forfeited their possessions in the United States upon the declaration of peace in 1783, but were compensated by the British government with the large grant on the St. John River, extending for several miles along the shore and as far back, which came to be called Spring Hill.

Robert and Christopher Murray, who remained in New York, were no more patriotic than Robert's wife. Perhaps the zealousness with which she embraced the cause of independence might have accounted for the rift in the family. Her reception of Generals Howe and Clinton and other British officers, whom she entertained at Murray Hill "with pleasant conversation and a profusion of cake and wine," while General Putnam and his division slipped out to the Heights of Harlem from the trap in which they had been caught in New York city, has left its impress upon the history of 1776. Robert Murray afterwards achieved distinction as a lawyer and was pitted

against Alexander Hamilton as counsel in the first newspaper libel suit tried in the United States. Murray Hill,
his farm on the outskirts of the city and the lake upon it
are no more. They have been engulfed by the advancing
tide of buildings but the name is still applied to the section
of the metropolis to which they gave place.

Relatives of the Murray family remained in London
and one of them, a cousin, Elizabeth Watson by name,
came to New Brunswick to visit the Loyalist brothers
at Spring Hill. At this time my father was in charge of
Colonel Allen's estate adjoining. Doubtless in the come
and go of life along the St. John the two were thrown
together. In any event Elizabeth Watson tarried long at
Spring Hill, they came to know each other, and in 1815,
several years after her arrival, they were married.

Although the Murrays had been divided in their
allegiance, their domestic friendships remained undisturbed.
Christopher and Robert, long after the feeling over the
rebellion of the colonies had subsided, came to Spring
Hill from time to time to visit their brothers; and my
mother, whose destinies had taken her to other places,
frequently rejoined the family circle. It was on one of
these occasions that I, as a small child playing about the
house with a donkey, fell under the eye of Christopher, by
avocation a broker in New York City. He had no children, and being, for one reason or another, attracted to
me, he proposed to my mother that he adopt me with the
understanding that I be made his heir. My mother,
however, did not fall in with this plan. I was destined
to come to the United States in another way.

Some time between 1820 and 1822, my father transferred his activities to an estate called Lincoln, nine miles
from Fredericton, a large tract of land granted to Colonel

Lemuel Wilmot, also a refugee from the states.[1] In this undertaking he assumed a larger measure of responsibility and had entire direction of the lumbering and farming operations carried on there, receiving as compensation a share of the proceeds. The Wilmot family played an important part in the affairs of New Brunswick. Allen Wilmot, the son of Colonel Wilmot, one of the most distinguished lawyers in Canada and for a time Governor of the province, spent his vacations at Lincoln while my father was in charge of the estate.

At this place my oldest sister, Margaret, my brother Andrew, and my sister Elizabeth Ann, were born.

After living at Lincoln for several years my father again moved still farther down the river to Maugerville,— one of the older settlements, laid out in 1762,— where he took charge of the estate of Colonel Miles.[2] This land was the most fertile in a region renowned for its fertility and produced from sixty to one hundred bushels of corn to the acre. Shortly after the arrival of the family there I was born on June 18, 1829.

It was not long after his removal to Maugerville that my father attracted the attention of Samuel Nevers,[3] Squire Nevers, one of the conspicuous figures in the early development of the lumbering industry along the St. John River, a man of large enterprise who had supplied

[1] Wilmot, Lemuel, of Long Island, New York; entered the service of the Crown and at the peace was captain in the loyal American regiment. In 1783 he settled on the river St. John, New Brunswick, where he continued to reside. He died near Fredericton in 1814. He received half pay. Hannah, his wife, a daughter of the Hon. Daniel Bliss, died in 1810. (Sabin.)

[2] Miles, Elijah. In 1783 he settled in New Brunswick. He was a judge of the Court of Common Pleas, a colonel in the militia, and a member of the House of Assembly. He died at Maugerville, in the County of Sunbury, at the age of seventy-nine. (Sabin.)

[3] The Nevers family was of original Puritan stock and first settled in Woburn, Massachusetts, in 1666. They were original grantees of the settlement at Maugerville.

masts to enable Francklin, Hazen and White, the pioneer lumbering firm of the province, to fulfill their contract with the Royal Navy. He engaged my father to manage the varied and extensive operations he carried on at Hartland, about eight miles up the river from Maugerville, where he had built a huge house, known as Nevers Castle, and established a sawmill, gristmill and oatmeal-mill at the mouth of the Becaguimec River. In addition there was a greenhouse, a supply store and warehouse; and the activities of the place included farming, lumbering, and vessel-building.

Squire Nevers, who in more modern nomenclature would have been rated as an operator of great importance, according to the standard of the time, eventually suffered reverses and the fruits of his earlier success were dissipated. One of his descendants many years afterward sought employment of me in Wisconsin. My brother, S. M. Stephenson, of Menominee, Michigan, was born at Hartland on Christmas Day, 1832, and was a namesake of Squire Nevers.

We lived at Hartland for four or five years, at the end of which time my father, desirous of taking up an independent career, purchased from Squire Nevers a farm at Greenfield, twenty-five miles farther up the river, near the mouth of the Shiktehawk. Here my brother Robert was born, and here my mother died on New Year's Day, 1838, when I was less than nine years old, leaving six children, four boys and two girls.

CHAPTER II

Life along the St. John — Farming, lumbering, and vessel-building —
Home life and the schools — "Frolics" — The Aroostook War —
Beginnings of the lumbering industry — Masts for the Royal
Navy — Ton timber — Disappearance of the forests — Necessity
for husbanding resources.

L IFE along the St. John River during my early boyhood was full of activity; and in the forest or on the
farm every moment of the day, from dawn until
twilight, was given up to labor. The period was one of
abounding prosperity. The demand for timber from abroad,
especially for masts and spars, was apparently unlimited
and as the forests were cleared away the fertile soil, especially in the intervales, yielded rich harvests. These opportunities were the goal for an unending stream of immigrants
principally from Ireland and Scotland.

The St. John River, the broad thoroughfare to the
sea, was a constantly shifting panorama of the industries
which prevailed along its banks, from the wilderness above
to the city at its mouth where the tide rolls in with resistless energy from the Bay of Fundy. At Hartland
and Spring Hill I saw, as a child, the products of the forest
go by in an endless stream of rafts, the towboats laden
with supplies for the farms, the canoes of the Indians and
white men, the pirogues of the Acadians carrying to
market the woolen garments made from their own flocks of
sheep and maple sugar obtained in the woods. Even at
night it was not still. Through the darkness flared the

flambeaux of the fishermen, the lure of the salmon of which its waters yielded rich harvest.

The lands bordering upon the river from the mouth to Grand Falls, over which I have seen huge logs plunge like chips in a torrent, were considered from the point of view of the time a well settled area. Villages and small settlements were numerous and at intervals between them were small water-mills, taverns and stores at which the farmers obtained their supplies. In addition to the common occupations, farming and lumbering, vessel-building had become a well established industry. It was carried on at Hartland, Squire Nevers' place, and at Taylortown and Sheffield — the one above, the other below, Maugerville. It is recorded that Benedict Arnold, who took refuge in the province and lived for a time at St. John, came into possession by not altogether honorable means of the Lord Sheffield, the first ship built on the river. As far back as 1800, sixty-seven ships were launched on the St. John; and at one time during that period two hundred square rigged vessels lay in St. John harbor awaiting cargoes.

I have, of course, no direct recollection of Maugerville, where I was born. It has since shrunk to a quiet hamlet, and the house of Colonel Miles, where I first saw the light of day, undermined by the river, has been obliterated. The same melancholy fate has overtaken the Allen and Murray estates at Spring Hill. Only a few of the buildings which were standing in my time, including the two little Episcopal churches at which the people of the neighborhood worshiped, remain.

My earliest experiences were at Hartland, Squire Nevers' place, and on the farm at Greenfield. The landmarks most distinctly fixed in my memory in this vicinity were

Charles McMullen's "castle," a short distance below Hartland, Robert Carr's store and hotel on the main river near Greenfield, Tupper's store and the gristmill and blacksmith shop on Buttermilk Creek. However unimportant they might appear from the latter-day point of view, in the social and industrial scheme of things that prevailed in New Brunswick during the early part of the last century these supply stores, mills, taverns, and blacksmith shops were institutions of much consequence from which the activity of the neighborhood radiated.

For those who were old enough life meant, at this time, little more than hard work. My father gave his attention to the farm during the summer-time. In the winter and spring he was away in the woods, lumbering or logging. This routine was followed by most of the men on the upper St. John; and not a few of them, when the long day was over, came home to thresh grain and attend to the needs of their live stock. Many times while driving homeward after a belated excursion in the neighborhood I heard the sound of the beating flails coming through the darkness from the barns along the roadside.

Our manner of living was simple. There was little leisure and the luxuries were few, but our activity in the woods and on the river kept us in bounding health and good spirits and we did not regard our lot as at all difficult. Stoves were, in this region at least, unknown. The big open hearth, with its blazing logs, its pots and kettles, was the center of domestic activity. Beside it stood the dyeing pot, the large old-fashioned spinning wheel, and the other crude implements of the day with which the wool from the sheep — of which every farm maintained a flock, large or small — was carded, colored, and spun to be woven into cloth.

Public schools had not yet been established. The education of us children was committed to the charge of two Irish schoolmasters who taught with the aid of a birch rod and, as part compensation, were received as boarders and lodgers in the households of their pupils, going from one to another in succession. Even this rudimentary schooling was limited. As soon as a boy was old enough to share the pressing burden of labor his attention was absorbed by the farm or the forest, and the girls were called upon to perform some of the manifold household duties including carding, spinning, and weaving. Under the rigid rule of necessity they even made their hats out of braided wheat straw, in which art they became adept, and a modest ribbon for adornment was counted a valuable treasure. I remember distinctly the gravity of the investigation that followed the disappearance of one when I was a small boy.

The general diversion of the period was the "frolic," a neighborhood affair combining industry with pleasure corresponding to the "bee" in New England. There were "frolics" for mowing and reaping, for carding wool, quilting, clearing the forest, and hauling and raising barns,— almost every kind of work that could be carried on collectively with one's neighbors. The host, as beneficiary of the concerted effort, provided refreshments as elaborate as the modest scale of living afforded, among which, for the men, was a generous supply of rum, the favorite beverage of the time.

About this time, 1837, during the hay-making season, I set out one morning with one of our neighbors named Campbell, a vigorous old Irishman whose sympathies were with the Unionist cause, to cut out from his flock grazing on the commons three or four sheep which were to be slaughtered to provide mutton for the men working in the fields. It was a warm day and the work of rounding up the animals strenuous, and we sat down on the grass by the roadside to rest. Campbell, then an old man, propped against a tree, took from his pocket an Irish newspaper,— the only medium through which we received news of what was going on in the old world,— which must have been several weeks old at least, as it was brought by sailing vessel, adjusted his heavily rimmed spectacles and proceeded to read aloud to himself. Lying beside him, with one eye on the sheep, I listened attentively. In his slow and deliberate fashion entirely oblivious of my presence he read of the death of William IV and the accession of Queen Victoria, then eighteen years of age, to the throne of Great Britain and Ireland.

After my mother's death I was left to a large extent to follow my own inclinations, as my father was away much of the time in the woods and the only parental authority we recognized reposed in my elder sister. Perhaps in my vagaries I covered a larger field than other small boys because of my comparative freedom, and wandered more or less at will over the neighborhood. But I was in no wise different. I frequented the swimming-hole by a cedar tree which I visited in 1852, 1856, 1880, 1894, and 1903, and fished in a small lake back of the farm at Greenfield with one of our neighbors, Andy McMonigle, who occasionally gave me an Irish fish hook,— all fish hooks seemed to be of Irish origin. If that were lost I fell back on a bent pin, which served very well, as the abundance of the fish made up for what I might have lacked in the way of tackle.

The most important historical event of which I have a clear recollection was the controversy in 1839 over the boundary between Maine and New Brunswick, sometimes called the Aroostook War. In the diminishing perspective of three quarters of a century this incident appears to have been of little consequence, but in the environment in which I lived it loomed large in its proportions and to the people of the province it was a matter of grave portent.

The region involved in the controversy was that in which my father lumbered and was generally known as Madawaska, the territory originally occupied by the Acadians when they were transferred from their earlier settlements along the St. John. Along the border there had always been more or less smuggling. In my boyhood I had known of such devices as trap doors in the bottom of sleighs which could be sprung permitting the loads to fall in the snow by the wayside when a revenue officer hove in sight. Disputes also arose over the ownership of timber and the crisis was finally precipitated by clashes between the civil authorities of the State of Maine and the Province of New Brunswick.

Under the shadow of war in 1839 lumbering operations in Aroostook County and along the upper St. John generally ceased. On March 1st eight hundred fusiliers arrived in St. John from Cork and five hundred British regulars were sent to Madawaska. The farmers and lumbermen of the vicinity under British jurisdiction were pressed into service to haul soldiers to Quebec where the garrison was being strengthened; and on both sides of the boundary the militia was held in readiness for war, trains of sleighs laden with soldiers and munitions stretching along the roads through the forests.

The Yankees erected a blockhouse on the Aroostook River called Fort Fairfield, and at the mouth of the Fish River, where I afterward lumbered with my father, was

Fort Kent, named for the Governor of Maine, whose fame
has survived in the slogan:

> "Maine went
> Hell bent
> For Governor Kent."

When hostilities threatened and the militia of New
Brunswick was called out, my father, as orderly sergeant,
went into service. These forces were quartered in an un-
finished church at Tobique where he, by reason of his rank,
occupied the pulpit. In the vicinity was also a force of
grenadiers, regular troops. Between the two there was
always more or less friction and ill feeling which was mani-
fested in frequent brawls and fights, and on one occasion
the grenadiers invaded the church in which the militia
was housed and were on the point of charging them under
arms when Colonel Nugent, their commanding officer,
arrived just in time to prevent what might have been a
serious encounter.

Both regulars and militiamen frequented Tibbetts's
tavern, about a mile up the Tobique River. One afternoon my father went to this place to warn two of his men,
John Laird and James McMonigle, to return to quarters
before their leave expired. Two grenadiers, who were
in the bar-room at the rear of the tavern drinking, went
out shortly after he entered and secreted themselves in
a hallway. When he passed a moment later they struck
him down with a handspike, leaving him lying unconscious
on the floor. Here he was discovered by McMonigle and
Laird who, after summoning aid, armed themselves with
pine clubs and set out in pursuit of the assailants.

They overtook them on the river bank a short distance from the tavern. Laird felled his man with a blow,
but McMonigle's club broke. He thereupon grappled

with the grenadier and in the struggle the two men rolled over and over, down the river bank to the ice below. Fortunately for McMonigle, he brought up on top and proceeded in a blind fury to beat the soldier with the remnant of his weapon until others intervened. As a penalty for the assault one of the grenadiers, after a trial, was transported to Botany Bay; the other died at St. John before he was sentenced. For six weeks my father was incapacitated and never fully recovered from the effects of the injury he sustained which, I have no doubt, shortened his life, although he was eighty-five years old when he died.

Some of the incidents of this period which I remember bore a less serious aspect. About this same time Stover Ryan, a Yankee,— whom I met a number of years afterward at Janesville, Wisconsin,— while hauling a small cannon on a sleigh, left his charge and went into a tavern to refresh himself. John Bradley, one of the men employed by my father, saw the unguarded piece and, stirred with patriotic fervor, set about to unlash it and drag it to a water hole in the ice on the river, where he purposed to consign it to watery oblivion. Before he succeeded Ryan appeared and he took to his heels. This was not the only one of Bradley's patriotic exploits. He also set fire to the Yankee blockhouse at Fort Fairfield, but the blaze was extinguished before much damage was done. The blackened logs remained, however, a monument to his prowess.

Fortunately, the war over the boundary was averted largely through the efforts of Sir John Harvey, Governor of New Brunswick, and General Winfield Scott. These men had become intimate friends through unusual circumstances. General Scott saved Sir John's life in the War of 1812 at the battle of Lundy's Lane, and not long after-

ward Sir John performed the same service for General Scott
at Quebec where, while a prisoner of war, he was set upon
by several Indian chiefs who were bent on killing him.
They were selected to take up preliminary negotiations
and signed a protocol at Augusta, Maine, on March 23,
1839. Subsequently, in accordance with the terms of the
Webster-Ashburton treaty, the controversy was submitted
to arbitration and the boundary was fixed by the King of
the Netherlands.

The part played by Daniel Webster, then Secretary
of State, in the negotiations made him the target indirectly
for much bitter criticism. When President Harrison, by
whom he was appointed, died and was succeeded by President Tyler, Webster did not resign with the other members of the cabinet. For this he was denounced by his
party colleagues, the Whigs, whom Tyler had antagonized,
and virulent attacks were made upon him. After the
boundary controversy had been settled he explained pub-
licly, in a speech at Faneuil Hall, that he had been performing a patriotic duty by remaining at his post against
his will until the treaty negotiations had been completed
and turned the guns of his oratory upon those who had
been criticizing him for his action.

At this time the dominating industry along the St.
John River which overshadowed every other activity was
lumbering. It was to the forests that the province owed
in greatest measure its prosperity and its rapid development. From the very outset of its history they attracted
the attention of explorers. French and English naviga-
tors skirting the shores of the St. John River observed
that the trees were of a size far greater than those yielded
by the forests of the old world, and because of their straight
trunks and great height were incomparable for masts and

spars. Nowhere else, it was thought, could such timber be obtained, and the constantly increasing size of sailing vessels demanded loftier masts for their equipment.

When the English dominion was extended into Canada, after the battle of Quebec, the English government itself adopted a plan prohibiting the cutting of pine trees within three miles of the shores of the river St. John. Later surveyors of the Crown were sent into the woods to select trees suitable for masts which they marked with broad arrows. Afterward this plan was abandoned and a law was passed allowing a bounty for trees beyond a certain size. This, I believe, is still in effect, although it is no longer observed.

Immediately after the Revolution, when the supply from the colonies was cut off, the British government entered into contracts with New Brunswick lumbermen to provide masts for the Royal Navy, and two or three firms took up the work. The arrival of the first cargo at Halifax on the way to England in a navy transport was considered of such importance that it was announced to the British Secretary of State by the Lieutenant-Governor.

The rivalry to obtain suitable trees was keen among these early operators. The importance which the industry assumed may be gathered from the Francklin, Hazen and White correspondence, according to which success was measured in terms of the number and size of logs obtained. "I take this opportunity," Peabody, one of the agents, wrote to his firm in 1782, "of acquainting you that I have the offer of about 20 sticks from Samuel Nevers and Mr. Tapley. The sticks is well sized, one mast of 30 inches & one 23 inch Yard, and others of lower sizes. I finished hauling masts at Roosagwanis last thursday. Got out 37 sticks without any misfortune, & tomorrow morning shall move our Teams to Glazier's, where I expect to git out 40 or 45 sticks."

With Samuel Nevers and Sherman Tapley, then engaged in the masting industry, my father became associated later on; and in this environment I grew up as a boy. It was but natural under the circumstances that I should have been attracted to the forest and, whether I liked it or not, that my experiences should have taken me in the way of lumbering. As it was I submitted without reluctance and learned willingly many lessons which I was able to apply to great advantage in the West, where I hauled masts and spars for many of the vessels on the Great Lakes. Even offers of a university career did not divert me. For nearly four score years I have held constantly to this course into which my destiny guided me.

The greater proportion of merchantable timber at this time was ton timber or hewn timber, although some lumber was sawed in the small water-mills along the river and at St. John. A ton or load was twelve inches square and forty feet long. Sometimes as much as eight or ten tons were obtained from a single pine tree and timber from twenty to thirty inches square was exceedingly valuable. In this form it was transported, in ships built especially for that purpose, to England, Ireland, and Scotland, where it was in great demand, and whip-sawed by hand.

To digress for a moment: I doubt whether anyone has a keener realization than I of the extent to which the timber resources of the United States are being exhausted. When I was a boy the thousands of rafts floated down the St. John River gave evidence of the wealth of the forests that were falling before the axe of the colonist and the lumberman. Later, when I went to Maine with my father, the upper reaches of the Penobscot poured a constant stream of logs down to the busy mills between Oldtown and Bangor. What the great stretch of continent to the westward was to yield in the way of timber was as yet a closed book, some of the pages of which I myself turned from day to day in the way of work and experience. It fell to my lot in some measure to blaze a way through some of the most extensive forests that have added millions to the wealth of the country and contributed more than can be easily estimated to its upbuilding.

Within the limits of a single lifetime, a rather long lifetime, perhaps, what once seemed to be illimitable stretches of virgin forest in New Brunswick, in Maine, in Wisconsin and Michigan, have melted away before the westward tide of settlement. The scarcity of timber that seemed so remote then is now ominously close. I have seen the pine forests of Wisconsin and Michigan, untracked by white men, disappear, the hard woods going and the developed farms spreading over what was not many years ago the heart of the wilderness.

East of the Rocky Mountains timber has been cut so rapidly that there is now a scarcity of raw material for lumber, ties, pulpwood, and other products. The question of reforestation is upon us. Devastated areas must be replanted and the resources that still remain to us husbanded. This, of course, will be a slow process. From now until our efforts have yielded fruit we must look to Canada, where there is an immense wilderness of forest north of Lake Superior and west of Hudson Bay, for lumber, pulp and pulpwood. From this region the eastern portion of the United States can be supplied, and for this reason I believe there should be no tariff on lumber or any raw material coming from Canada. As a matter of fact, I am in favor of the free admission of all raw material.

Twenty-five years ago the Menominee River region was producing more logs than any other place in the world, between seven and eight hundred million feet a year, and many of the more experienced lumbermen were reaping the harvest that had been awaiting the axe from immemorial times. If the prediction had been made then that the pine timber would have been exhausted in a quarter of a century, it would have been received with derision. Yet this has come to pass.

There are still great forests in California, Oregon, and Washington, but I now venture to make the prophecy that in another twenty-five years this supply will be practically exhausted if restrictive measures are not imposed upon the activities of the lumbermen. What with the cutting and the waste, the devastating forest fires, and the persistent and resistless extension of the cultivated land areas, timber will be scarce and we shall be obliged to look to the British possessions for our supply.

CHAPTER III

*Beginning of my lumbering career in 1840 — Camp on the Shikte-
hawk — Routine of the logging camps — Difficulties of contractors — Family removes to Aroostook County, Maine —
Conditions in Aroostook and Yankee operations — Jefferson
Sinclair, Napoleon of Maine lumbering industry — Use of
oxen in logging — Log drive down the St. John River in 1844 —
Journey to Bangor over old stage route.*

IN August, 1840, when I was little more than eleven
years old, I began my career in lumbering. With
seven men,— five of whom had blackened eyes, evidence of the rum-drinking and fighting commonly indulged
in by the Irish, Scotch, and English along the river at
this time,— I set out for my father's camp on the Mira-
michi road, six miles up the Shiktehawk River, about
ten miles from my home in Greenfield. I rode a black
horse with which we "snaked" our two canoes around
the rocks where the current was swift, and twice swam
across intersecting streams clinging to the hames of my
mount.

At the camp were fifteen men, with fourteen horses,
felling the trees, hewing them into ton timber and piling
them on rollways on the banks of the river whence they
were floated down the St. John for the export trade. In
accordance with the system of the time Sherman Tapley,
an associate of Squire Nevers, as the "supply man," advanced the equipment and provisions for the camp. My
father as contractor had full charge of and was responsible
for the operations carried on.

The winter of 1840 and 1841 was unusually rigorous. The snow was seven feet deep, and whether for this or some other reason the country was overrun with a horde of wolves which, it was supposed, had migrated from the ice-bound wilderness to the north in search of food. At the camp they did not molest us, but they invaded the sheep folds at the farms in packs and slaughtered the unfortunate animals by the scores. Some of the poorer families for lack of secure stables were obliged to take their small flocks into their houses at night for safe keeping.

Work at the camp moved according to a well-measured routine. The men arose shortly before daybreak and went to work in the woods on snowshoes, beginning as soon as the light was sufficient to enable them to see clearly. Except for the brief interval of rest at midday for dinner which I brought to them, they kept at it steadily until nightfall, when they returned to camp. Being too tired for diversion, as a rule, they went to bed shortly after supper. So life moved for them day after day until the approach of spring unlocked the fast-frozen streams, and the timber was floated down to market. The only respite from labor was afforded by Sunday, and on that day axes were ground, repairs made, and the camp set in order for operations during the week.

To me was assigned the duty of cooking. Although not very proficient, I managed well enough, as our fare was limited to pork, beans, bread, molasses, tea, and dried apples,— not a well diversified diet but as good as could be obtained under the circumstances. The men were satisfied mainly, perhaps, because the time did not afford a higher standard by which they might measure the short-comings of their own lot. Nor did their health suffer for lack of luxuries, edible or otherwise. Sickness was rare.

In my long experiences in the woods in New Brunswick, in Maine, and in later years, in Wisconsin and Michigan, I discovered that ordinary ailments and diseases were phenomena of community life and that their prevalence was largely in proportion to the complexities of the modern way of living. In the isolated camps in the pine forests they had no place.

Logging and timber making, of course, had its dangers. During this same winter one of the men of our camp, Kinney Landers, was killed, and another, named Hoyt, was injured while breaking out a rollway. Both men, citizens of the United States, were pinned under the rolling logs and Landers was crushed to death. For the funeral, I remember, the activities of the camp were suspended for three or four days when time was most valuable. There were also many cuts and gashes due to the slipping of axes on the frozen timber, but infection of the wounds was extremely rare — I do not remember a case of what has been called blood-poisoning — and recovery rapid.

Most of the lumbering at this time was done by men who, like my father, contracted to fell the trees and hew the logs into square timber. Capital was scarce and the contractors generally were obliged to obtain their supplies on credit, a condition that was unfortunate for those who were most active in the industry. Unscrupulous capitalists, in many instances, took every advantage of the harsh debtors' laws to acquire possession of the fruits of the labor of the men who suffered hardship and privation in the forest and upon whom the burden of production rested most heavily. When the timber had been cut the creditors, under cover of the drastic law, swooped down upon the contractors and seized it for debt before it could be delivered. The contractor himself was thrown into a debtor's cell. Some of the largest lumbering firms in Canada resorted to this practice, which became a positive evil, and hundreds of the most efficient lumbermen in New Brunswick to escape the sheriff fled across the border and took refuge in Maine, where they contributed much to the prosperity and upbuilding of the country.

In the winter of 1840 and 1841 one Purdy, of the firm of Purdy and Dibble, storekeepers, arrived at our camp with a deputy sheriff of the county, named Craven, on their way to arrest William Rogers, a neighboring contractor and to seize his timber and equipment for debt. My father's sympathies were naturally with Rogers and, while acting as host to Craven and Purdy, who remained over night, he sent a boy, William Coulter, out surreptitiously to warn him of their coming. Rogers entrenched himself behind natural barriers by driving his horses up the byroads and blocking the main thoroughfare by felling trees across it. When Craven and Purdy arrived at his camp on foot they found it deserted and returned home without accomplishing their purpose. Before they could renew their attempt Rogers succeeded in making arrangements to tide himself over the difficulty.

Craven was a spectacular figure in the neighborhood, a duelist of some renown and a picturesque character. A few days before he had visited our camp he had an encounter with William Dustin, at Scotch Corners, just outside of Woodstock, and was slightly wounded under the arm. Ultimately, however, his bravado resulted in his downfall. A few years after this incident he went to California, joining the early rush to the goldfields, and was lynched, I believe, by the vigilantes in 1849.

In 1843, when I was fourteen years of age, my father went to Maine and settled in township number eleven, in

Aroostook County, at a place now known as Ashland,[1] where he purchased a farm. Shortly afterward he became a citizen of the United States.

Aroostook County, bordering upon New Brunswick and drained partly by the tributaries of the St. John River, was as much a timber region as the adjoining territory though more sparsely settled. The Yankees, whose operations along the headwaters of the Penobscot had made Oldtown with Bangor the most important lumber producing center of the United States, had already penetrated the Madawaska region, where their activities had precipitated the boundary dispute of 1839. They worked in the same camps with the Canadians, floated their logs down the Aroostook and other rivers into the St. John, and at this time began to compete with the New Brunswick firms in the production of square timber for export.

The territory comprising the State of Maine had been originally a part of the State of Massachusetts, to which

[1] Conditions in Aroostook County are naïvely set forth as follows by E. Holmes, who made a survey of the region in that year under commission from the state of Maine:

"Should you advise me to go to Aroostook? is a question often put. Before answering this, I would use the characteristic privilege of asking, Who are you?

"If you are already well situated — have a good farm — live in a pleasant neighborhood, and are blessed with the common goods and chattels necessary for the well being and happiness of your family, stay where you are — go neither east nor west. Are you a man of feeble health, with little capital, unable to undergo the severe trials of subduing the forest, and unable to hire? It would not be advisable for you to go there. Are you idle — lazy — shiftless and vicious? Go not thither. Better stay where (if you cannot reform) almshouses and prisons are more abundant to administer to your necessities, or to ensure your safe keeping. Are you in straitened circumstances, but in good health, with a robust and hardy family of children to assist you? Go to the Aroostook. If possible, take a supply of provisions with you till you can get a crop — select a good lot of land, be prudent and industrious, and in three years you can look around upon your productive acres and your well filled garners with satisfaction. Are you a young man just starting in life, but with no capital, save a strong arm — good courage, and a *narrow axe?* Go to the Aroostook; attend assiduously and carefully to your business; select a lot suitable for your purpose, and with the common blessings of providence, you will, in a few years, find yourself an independent freeholder, with a farm of your own subduing, and with a capital of your own creating."

was reserved, when the division was made, the timber on every odd township. Among others the firm of Sinclair, Jewett and March, one of the oldest and largest of the lumbering concerns of Bangor, which had operated extensively along the Penobscot, purchased tracts of this stumpage in Aroostook County and established a number of camps for the production of square timber.

With the management of the business of the firm Jewett, a capitalist, and March, a banker, had little to do. The directing spirit of the enterprise was Jefferson Sinclair, one of the most prominent practical lumbermen of a time when lumbering was the most important of Maine's varied industries. In this field Mr. Sinclair, to whom I was to owe so much of whatever success I have achieved, was without equal. His operations were very extensive and he directed them with a masterfulness and finality of decision that made him the Napoleon of lumbering in the chief seat of the industry in the United States. His logging camps were scattered over a large area in Aroostook County, in the watersheds of the St. John as well as of the Penobscot, and his logs and timber were floated down both rivers.[1]

The boom at Oldtown, probably the greatest of its kind in the world at the time, where the logs coming down

[1] In a tattered copy of "Sketches of Old Town," the title page of which is missing, I find the following biographical reference to Mr. Sinclair:

"Came here in connection with Rufus Dwinel; was boom master some five years; was quite extensively engaged in lumbering business; was an energetic and enterprising man, and was the successor to John B. Morgan as president of the Bank of Old Town. During his administration of the bank affairs, the financial crisis of 1837 reached its culmination, and this bank, with many others, succumbed to the force of the storm. His style of doing business was like this: He and Purinton had rented some shore to lay logs upon; some one had hitched logs there, and Purinton had posted a notice requesting the owners to remove them. After the notice was up, St. Clair added the words, 'or they will all be moved at once.'"

In the same volume it is recorded that in 1838 Jefferson Sinclair was chosen a Selectman of Old Town.

the Penobscot were sorted for the mills which lined the banks of the river from that point down to Bangor at the head of tidewater, was a monument to his constructive genius. He built it in company with Rufus Dwinel, thereby establishing a precedent that has been followed on all of the important lumbering streams of the country up to the advent of the railroads.

In logging the Yankees were probably more expert than the Canadians but had less experience in making ton timber, and for this purpose Mr. Sinclair engaged men who had done work of this kind on the St. John. My father was one of these. He entered into a contract with Sinclair, March and Jewett, and during the winters of 1842, 1843, and 1844 employed between twenty and thirty men in the region around Eagle and Portage lakes on the road from the Aroostook River to the mouth of Fish River. Here I received my first practical experience in lumbering and acquired the knowledge of logging which was to be of incalculable value to me in Wisconsin and Michigan.

From these camps, where men were trained to meet the rigors of the wilderness and to overcome the obstacles that lumbering entailed, hundreds of pioneers scattered over the timber regions of the West. They were a hardy lot, mostly of English, Irish, or Scotch birth or parentage, who mastered the variety of trades required by their occupation and were at home alike in forest, on farm, and on stream. There were in the older region also a number of French-Canadians among whom were what we designated "jumpers" or "jumping Frenchmen," the victims, to all appearances, of a nervous ailment which subjected them to the whims of sensory impulses. At a sharp command or upon hearing a sudden noise or being struck a sharp blow, they jumped spasmodically, some-

FROM A DAGUERREOTYPE

JEFFERSON SINCLAIR

times with disastrous consequences to themselves. I
have known them to jump out of a boat into the water
when told unexpectedly to do so. Dr. George M. Beard,
a physician, who conducted a series of experiments with
them a number of years ago, said of them: "These jumpers
have been known to strike their fists against a red-hot
stove; they have been known to jump into fire as well
as into water; indeed, no painfulness or peril of position
has any effect on them; they are as powerless as apoplec-
tics or hysterics, if not more so."

According to the methods of logging which prevailed
in Maine, when a tree was felled a pathway was cleared
through the deep snow to the main road and the log with
one end chained to a sled was dragged from the stump.
The hauling was done by teams of three yoke of oxen, the
driving of which was one of the most difficult and remun-
erative accomplishments of the lumbering craft. Ox
teamsters, who were looked upon as persons of a higher
category by the swampers and axemen, were paid in some
cases, as much as sixty dollars a month, while the foreman
of the camp received only from twenty-six to thirty dollars
and their wages were little short of munificent according to the scale then maintained.

The use of oxen in logging can be traced back directly
to the period before the American Revolution when the
English and French governments began to draw upon the
forests of Maine and New Brunswick for white pine for
masts and spars. Only the oxen trained for that purpose,
with their slow, steady pull, were strong enough to drag the
huge trunks, some of them more than three feet in diameter
and a hundred feet in length, out of the woods. In 1815
and later it was the practice in Maine to drive them even
singly in hauling timber to the rivers.

In my father's camps I set out to master the art, for such it was, learning not only to drive the oxen but to train them. This latter task required about two months for a team of six and could be accomplished at all only by the exercise of the greatest patience and forbearance. The animals were driven with a goad stick, about four feet long, five eighths of an inch thick at the large end and a half-inch at the smaller, with a brad about a half-inch in length. Outside of Maine and New Brunswick whips were commonly used.

The rivalry among the drivers in the Maine forests, of whom there were hundreds, perhaps thousands, was extraordinarily keen. Contests in hauling trees or starting boats laden with stone held as important a place in the diversions of the day as the more athletic sports or races of the present. Fortunately, I made the most of my opportunity. The knowledge I acquired stood me in good stead in after years when we did most of the masting on the upper lakes. At Escanaba, Michigan, sixty-five years ago I ranked among the best drivers; and I took, and still take, a great deal of pride in that accomplishment.

In 1844 I went down the Fish River and the St. John on the first log drive of large proportions in those waters. Before this time timber and logs were brought down from the upper river loose in small quantities to a point below Grand Falls where they were gathered together into small rafts. These were poled as far as Spring Hill, at the head of tidewater, made into larger rafts, and floated down with the tide to St. John.

The Yankee lumbermen first adopted the practice of bringing the timber down the rivers loose in large quantities and established the methods of log driving which were followed in the West. Here again I was to profit by my experience. The lessons I learned from Jefferson Sinclair, who built the boom at Oldtown and superintended this first great drive down the St. John, I applied to great advantage on the Menominee River, which came to be as important in the fifties and later as the Penobscot had been before and produced hundreds of millions of feet of timber every year.

On the St. John drive there were two crews, each consisting of one hundred men, one under the direction of George Lincoln, the other under Henry Colton. My function was to serve as "cookee," or assistant to the cook, in which capacity I accompanied Colton's crew. The position was not so difficult as might be supposed. The cook, a personage of some importance in the environment in which he moved, was not merely my superior but a very good friend. For three months, or until the drive was completed, we tented together, and during our leisure moments I taught him to read and write while he taught me French. Colton, who afterwards went to Pennsylvania, where he had charge of the boom at Williamsport, also took me under his special protection and asked me to come and live with him. We constituted, if not a picturesque, at least a very congenial trio.

The course of the drive was through Portage, Eagle, and Long lakes to the mouth of Fish River and thence down the St. John. In the hazards encountered,— the breaking of jams and the passage of dangerous rapids,— I, of course, did not share. None the less the journey was eventful. The timber was to have been collected at Glazier's boom, seven miles below Fredericton, and rafted the remainder of the distance; but the boom proved unequal to the strain put upon it and broke, and we were compelled to continue our operations down to St. John.

This enabled me to secure my first glimpse of a city and the vessels at anchor in the harbor. It was taken, however, under the protection of some of the members of the crew, as the belligerent Irish boys around the wharves were only too glad of an opportunity to war upon an unsuspecting lad from the country who undoubtedly indicated by his actions that the environment was a novel one. It was July by the time we returned to Aroostook.

I came in contact, more or less, at the camps and on the drive with Mr. Sinclair and, fortunately for me, attracted the great lumberman's attention. This was the beginning of the friendly interest he took in me which was to exercise the most potent influence in the molding of my career. In the fall of that year, 1844, Mr. March fell ill at Ashland. As soon as he had recovered his strength sufficiently he set out, with Mrs. March, for his home in Bangor, and I was commissioned to accompany him as driver with the understanding that I was to be taken into the Sinclair household after our arrival. From Ashland we went to Mattawamkeag and from there down to Bangor, following the old stage road.

This was a famous thoroughfare, through one of the busiest sections of the United States, skirting the Penobscot River. The stages, staunch Concord coaches elaborately finished, were the highest achievement of the craft of the wagon builder and seated more than a score of passengers. The drivers, jauntily attired and wearing kid gloves, were persons of imposing presence. From their lofty position on the box, where they manipulated the reins of the six horses with impressive dexterity, they surveyed the traveling public with an air of tolerant superiority. Nor did they stoop to the care of horses. This function was performed by the hostlers at the stations every ten or fifteen miles along the route.

Eight years later, in 1852, I made the journey from Holton to Mattawamkeag over the military road and down to Bangor over the same route. On this occasion there were two coaches, one carrying twenty-seven passengers, the other an extra with the surplusage of travelers following close at our heels. The driver, named Crockett, turned the reins of the first coach over to me when we arrived at Oldtown, while he went back to take the passengers in the extra coach to their destinations, and I drove in state up to the Wadleigh Hotel, where a hostler came to take charge of the horses.

These drivers were constantly undertaking errands for the people living along the stage route. Women hailed them as they passed and commissioned them to buy calico, thread, or other articles in Oldtown or Bangor, which they delivered on the return trip. Crockett told me that he frequently spent several hours shopping in the evening in Bangor to purchase a variety of things to be delivered to persons along the route the following day.

At Oldtown, at the head of the rapids in the Penobscot, we came to the sawmills operated by water power. For the last ten miles of the journey the banks were lined with these establishments, the flower of the great lumber industry which prevailed there for seventy years.

At Bangor, then a city of twenty-five thousand people and one of the most important business centers in New England, I lived with the Marches for several months until Mr. Sinclair came down in the following spring. This was a turning point in my career, although I might not have been aware of it at the time. It marked the end of my experiences in the older environment of New Brunswick and Maine and the beginning of a series of events which were to take me away from my family into what was then the far West, where the country was in the making. In the interim, however, I saw something of the life of the city as a member of the household of Mr. Sinclair, who included me in his own family circle and treated me as a son, then and afterward taking advantage of every opportunity to put me forward in the way of experience and teach me the lessons to which, more than anything else, I owe my success in the field of practical lumbering. Mrs. Sinclair, too, looked after me with maternal solicitude and sympathy.

For a time I was able to resume the schooling which had been cut short by the exigencies of life in New Brunswick. I went to Miss Merrill's, on State Street, for several months, where I profited, no doubt, by coming into contact with the boys of the neighborhood. But the other aspects of Bangor were more fascinating to me. The shipping in the harbor was absorbingly interesting and under the spell of the romance of the wharves I conceived the ambition to become a sailor, which I sought to achieve afterward on the Great Lakes. The idea was encouraged by Mrs. March's brother, who had sailed before the mast, and Captain Eustis, the owner of a ship, who lived opposite the Sinclairs on State Street. The former taught me how to splice ropes and tie sailors' knots. The latter proposed that I ship on his vessel as a cabin boy with his son George, promising that we would have no other duties than to keep his cabin swept and clean. Every bit of knowledge I picked up of the handling of the big square-riggers, which then shed luster upon Maine's commercial greatness, I garnered carefully; and even the fleet of lobster boats and fishing vessels, which came close to the heart of the city, absorbed my attention. Lobsters at this time were especially abundant. They were hawked about the streets in barrows and the largest of them could be purchased for five cents, with pepper and salt, if one were minded to eat them on the spot.

These experiences were of short duration, a fleeting glimpse of the city as I went from one wilderness to another. Before the year was out I was to start again for the unsettled country.

CHAPTER IV

*Departure with Sinclairs for Milwaukee in 1845 — Journey from
Bangor to Boston and Albany — Discomforts of railway travel
— Inland voyage over Erie Canal — We encounter storms on
Lakes Erie, Huron, and Michigan — Milwaukee seventy years
ago — Immigration—Difficulties of pioneering.*

MR. SINCLAIR, in 1841, had made a trip to Wisconsin, the possibilities of which were then just beginning to dawn upon the people of the eastern portion of the United States, and purchased a quantity of land four miles from Racine at a place now called Mt. Pleasant. In 1845 he sold his interest in the firm of Sinclair, March and Jewett to his partners and prepared to go west.

One morning in October he called me into his room and told me of his intention, offering me one hundred and sixty acres of land, with a house, teams and other farm equipment if I would go with him and live with him until I was twenty-one years old. To a boy of sixteen this was a matter of the gravest importance. The proposal appealed to me. It offered opportunities for my own advancement and had a sufficient cast of adventure to stimulate my imagination and I was disposed to accept it. Before making a decision, however, I drove to Aroostook county to see my father and talk over the venture with him. With some reluctance he consented to my departure thinking at the time that he would follow me the next year. As it happened he did not go to Wisconsin until seventeen years later, in 1863. What this parting meant to him may be gathered from a letter I received from him under date of April 2, 1846.

"Dear Isaac," he wrote, "I have done very well this winter. You can tell Mr. Sinclair that I made and hauled 11 hundred sticks of timber on 13 in the range and camped in George Lincoln's old camp. With six horses we commenced hauling the 20th of December and quit the 12th of March.— It commenced to rain about that time. The snow was very light here this winter, about two feet and a half all winter. I expect to start to you as soon as the last of June.— Samuel worked in the woods for us all winter and he has Mr. Bradley's note for thirty dollars besides what he got when he settled. I am in hopes we will have something handsome to take with us when we go. You may depend upon me going if God spares my health for I want once more to see my children together. If you do not think the place will suit me I want you to tell me, for this place is very good at present. Now Isaac, be a good boy and I hope the Lord will prosper you. No more at present. I remain your affectionate father until death."

Long before his wish could be gratified my brothers and many of the men I had known in our camps in Maine and New Brunswick had come after me to seek their fortunes in the Wisconsin and Michigan forests.

The journey from Bangor was an extraordinary one, judging from latter-day standards. After packing all of the furniture except the stoves,— including even the zinc bathtub, the first of its kind in Milwaukee,— we embarked on the steamer "Penobscot" for Boston about the middle of October, 1845. Among our chattels were two Concord buggies and two or three sets of logging harness.

The latter were afterwards duplicated in Milwaukee by the harness maker, George Dyer, and were the type of harness in use in the West to-day.

One of our fellow passengers on the steamer "Penobscot" was our neighbor, Captain Eustis, who was also on his way to Boston to take charge of his ship, on which he contemplated making two trips to Nova Scotia for coal. His proposal that I accompany him with his eldest son as cabin boy opened new vistas of adventure which even the trip to Wisconsin and the assurances of moderate success did not obscure. After much wavering and doubt I succumbed to the lure of the sea.

When the Sinclair family was safely lodged in the hotel in Boston, where we remained for twenty-four hours at the conclusion of the first stage of our journey, I slipped down to the docks; but neither Captain Eustis nor his vessel was to be found although I made an earnest search. Concealing my disappointment I went back to the hotel and when the family resumed their travels I went along with them. Then, as in many instances since, some benignant fate rescued me as I was about to turn into the wrong path, all of which has sometimes led me to believe that, after all, a special providence may be watching over our destinies. I do not know. One can only wonder.

From Boston we continued our journey on the Boston and Albany railroad, one of the important transportation lines of the country. To those who know nothing of railroad travel except the luxurious trains of the present day, the conditions of passenger traffic on these early lines are almost inconceivable, so rapid has been the improvement of railroads and equipment. The passenger coaches were very much like the freight cars of to-day, though much smaller, and in some respects, I have no doubt, much less comfortable. There were only two windows, about six-teen by twenty inches in size, on each side of the cars to afford light and air and such glimpses of the passing land-scape as we were able to take. The floors were carpeted and in place of modern upholstered seats were three-legged stools which would be moved about at will. In the middle of each side of the cars was a sliding door similar to those now in use on box cars.

The train ran on strap rails, the modern form of rail not having been invented until some years later, and the conductors and trainmen passed from car to car by means of foot and hand rails attached to the sides. Although the speed was far from excessive the jolting and swaying made one's seat on the stools more or less precarious and the conditions were such that we were relieved when we arrived at Albany where we were to take a canal boat for Buffalo.

After another brief respite we boarded the "Northern Light," of the Clinton Line, owned and operated by Captain Spencer, who was about sixty years of age. This was a passenger boat with berths arranged along the sides for the full length of the hull, with the exception of the cabin, and the management of it was largely a family affair. Captain Spencer supervised matters and did the cooking and the other members of the family performed various functions. Express passenger boats, which were more elaborately equipped and towed by horses at a trotting pace for the entire length of the canal, were just coming into vogue at this time.

This stage of our voyage consumed five days. At the outset it was so disagreeable that we threatened to dis-embark and take the train. There were between thirty and forty passengers crowded together in the narrow quarters with no privacy whatever day or night; and Mr. Sinclair found them so uncomfortable, having been accustomed to less rigorous conditions, that Captain Spencer, particularly responsive to the threat that we would leave and make the rest of the journey on the railroad, proposed that we share his quarters in the after cabin, which we did and for which we paid more than the usual fare.

After my experiences in the woods I was probably less inconvenienced than the other members of our party, including the Sinclair children, and adjusted myself to the unavoidable conditions with philosophic interest. I was especially sympathetic with the boys who drove the tow horses, whose lot struck me as being very hard. They worked practically day and night with only short intervals of rest taken on deck or wherever they could find a place to lie, seldom, if ever, took off their clothes and bore the brunt of the hardship of this mode of travel. They were always ready to yield their responsibilities to me and clamber aboard the boat to rest, and I found it diverting to ride the horses which controlled the progress of the "Northern Light." Whenever the stern of the vessel was veered to the bank of the canal to permit passengers to alight I was usually among those who took advantage of the opportunity, and out of a total journey of three hundred and sixty miles rode the horses, I think, for at least a hundred. During the last leg of the journey some of the impatient passengers bribed one of the boys to urge his mount to greater speed, a cardinal offense, and the lad was discharged upon our arrival at Buffalo.

The railroad, the New York Central, followed the line of the canal, so that my interest was stimulated not only by the nautical aspect of the trip but by the sight of steam transportation as well. On this occasion I saw, for the first time, a telegraph line, a very crude affair compared with the perfected systems of the present day. Not being initiated into the mysteries of electricity I was much puzzled when told that the telegraph was used to convey news. News I construed to be newspapers and, from a mechanical point of view, I could not understand how the conveyance for the papers cleared the projecting ends of the telegraph poles.

At Buffalo, then the western terminus of the railroads, we took passage on the steamer "Empire," one of the largest boats on the lakes, and set out on the final stage of our long and tedious journey. The vessel, an infinite improvement upon the congested quarters of the canal boat, had as officers Captain Howe, Robert Wagstaff, first mate, and August Bartholomew, second mate. Seven years later returning from a trip to the East with several young men whom I was taking out to work for me in the Michigan forests, I again stopped at Buffalo to take the steamer to Monroe, Michigan, to which point the railroad had been extended eastward from Chicago. The "Northern Indiana," upon which we were to sail, had sunk in a collision and the "Empire" was substituted for her. By this time Bartholomew had been promoted to command.

On both trips on this vessel we encountered bad weather. On the first we roughed a terrific gale on Lake Erie and were obliged to make harbor at Cleveland. Here two vessels also seeking refuge in the harbor went ashore and another, the "Ben Franklin," stove a hole in her side above the water line. We were much relieved when the storm abated and started on our way again but only to run into another gale on Lake Huron. This time we had to take refuge at Presque Isle, where we remained for two or three days. Thence we proceeded to Manitou Islands for a supply of wood for fuel.

While we were there the steamer "Oregon" put in and Captain Cotton, commanding the vessel, brought the information that there was a very high sea on in Lake Michigan. Our captain paid no heed to this warning and decided to go on without delay. If the fate which ruled over the Middle West reflected its mood in bad weather certainly our coming was most unpropitious. We got under way in a gale which blew from the northeast, and the vessel rolled and pitched to such an extent that I was more or less bewildered and many of the passengers, keeping close to the heaving staterooms, were awaiting in fear and trembling the end of what appeared to be their disastrous journey. On the following day, however, the captain, having convinced himself of the danger, put into Grand Haven where we remained for two days, until the storm had abated and the lake calmed down. From there we went to Milwaukee without further mishap and landed at the north pier, at the foot of Huron Street, on Wednesday morning, November 15, 1845.

We disembarked with no small measure of satisfaction, glad that our perils were behind us and took breakfast at the City Hotel, now known as the Kirby House, on the corner of Mason and East Water streets, which was owned and conducted by Daniel Wells, Jr., who had come to Milwaukee several years before. I must confess that the feeling with which I first contemplated the village,— it was hardly more than that,— was one of disappointment. The population was only a few thousands and there was nothing about it to give promise that it would, within little more than a half-century, become a city of more than four hundred thousand people. After Bangor, an old and busy center, the straggling houses and the people, many of them immigrants but lately arrived from Europe, seemed odd and far from attractive. At Bangor, too, English was spoken; in Milwaukee German seemed to be the common tongue.

At this time Wisconsin was still a territory and, if Milwaukee appeared to measure inadequately up to the standards set by New England, certainly there was no other settlement within the jurisdiction that offered any greater promise. The entire region was largely a wilderness in which Green Bay and possibly Prairie du Chien were the outposts. But the tide of immigration had set in. On some days during this period I saw as many as seven or eight hundred people land at Milwaukee on steamers from Buffalo, packing their belongings with them; and I have seen them by the hundreds in a vacant lot bargaining for cattle and wagons with which to begin life and establish a farm on the unbroken prairie.

These were the pioneers to whom the state owes very largely whatever it has achieved in the way of commerce, agriculture, and the industries; builders of the foundation upon which the structure of success has been reared. The task which confronted them was not an easy one. Land, it is true, was cheap. It could be purchased from the government for a dollar and a quarter an acre but it required a vigorous spirit to confront without quailing the hardships and privations necessary to bring it under cultivation. Sometimes their crops were killed by the excessive cold of the winters; sometimes they were burned by the drouth of the summers. When they did obtain a harvest, not infrequently the prices they received for their grain were so low as to afford them a bare existence, enough to struggle on in the hope that conditions would be better the following year.

The same was true of lumbering. The idea that the government was lavish in its bounty in selling farming and timber lands for little more than the cost of surveying them is of recent origin. At that time there seemed to be no limit to the area of arable soil and the resources of the forests were so vast that they had never even been estimated. No one counted himself wealthy because of the land he possessed. What made the value of the crops and the lumber was the labor expended upon them, hard, gruelling labor under adverse conditions and oftentimes with no return but a living.

To add to the complications capital was scarce, money was uncertain as a medium of exchange and wages were low. When we left Maine, Mr. Sinclair, who was accounted from the point of view of the time a wealthy man, brought with him a large amount of currency issued by the Veazy Bank of Bangor, one of the most important in New England. Ordinarily only gold was acceptable outside the radius of certain well-known banking institutions. I still possess the belt in which I carried a stock of the metal on my early trips to the East.

Milwaukee, in these days of wildcat banking, was also fortunate in having an institution which weathered the storm that wrecked many of the badly conducted private and state banks. This was really not a bank at all, but the Marine and Fire Insurance Company which, however, issued its notes and conducted a general banking business. It was owned and established by George Smith, a Chicago financier, who brought Alexander Mitchell over from Scotland to manage it. When the flood of wildcat currency was circulating throughout the West generally, the notes of the Marine and Fire Insurance Company were always redeemable in specie. Smith's operations laid the foundation of the great fortune now held by his heirs in New York.

For the person who had no capital the difficulty of attaining an independent footing was almost insurmountable. Men worked on the farms for eight dollars a month and board. Girls and women did general housework for seventy-five cents a week, the wage rate for the most proficient, and the measure of luxuries they enjoyed would put to shame many women of the present day who consider themselves unfortunate. In 1846 and 1847 men could be obtained to cut wood off North Point for twenty-five cents a cord and wages for this service were traded in at the general store. From twenty-five to fifty cents a cord was the rate for cutting, splitting, and piling hardwood. The splitting, not infrequently, was done by women.

The problem, therefore, of establishing a home in the new country with nothing to start on was a very serious one, and the fact that lands were cheap offered little encouragement in the face of the trials and privations and the uncertainty of ultimate success. Now that the land has been occupied and brought under cultivation and the forests for the most part cut, it is a habit of mind to exaggerate the advantages afforded by the government's bounty and to minimize the hardships of pioneering. Having gone through most phases of this period I am more inclined to the belief that the government obtained the best of the bargain and that the returns to the country at large were of incalculable value.

CHAPTER V

*Mr. Sinclair takes up lumbering and farming in Wisconsin —
School in Milwaukee — Plowing on the prairie — The Lovejoys
— Traffic on the Janesville road — Lodging houses — Lead
wagons from Galena fields — Hauling flour — "Ague and chill
fever" epidemics — Logging at Escanaba — Lumbering north
of Green Bay — Conditions on the northern peninsula of Michigan — Carrying mails in the wilderness — Timber cruising.*

THE only industries of consequence in the Territory
of Wisconsin were farming and lumbering, both of
which had just entered upon the period of rapid
development that constitutes an epoch in the exploitation
and expansion of the resources of the United States. The
one was the corollary of the other. As the prairies were
settled and towns and cities were established and enlarged,
lumber was required for building; and as the volume of
immigration pouring itself over the broad acres of the Middle West grew, the lumbermen pushed their way the more
energetically into the forests.

Both of these industries absorbed Mr. Sinclair's attention. In the neighborhood of Janesville he owned a large
tract of land, as yet in a virgin state, which he purposed
to bring under cultivation. From his brother-in-law, Mr.
J. B. Smith, afterward mayor of Milwaukee, he also acquired an interest in a sawmill at Flat Rock, now Escanaba,
Michigan.

The exigencies of the time left no opportunity for diversion or relaxation nor did we regard it as necessary to
recuperate from the effects of our long and trying journey.

There was much hard work ahead of us and we set about doing it without a moment's delay. The morning after our arrival at Milwaukee, Mr. Sinclair hired a horse and buggy and we drove to Racine, which he intended to make his home. Here he left me, returning to the city where, as it happened, he was obliged to remain for four weeks because of the illness of his children. During this time I lived at the Congress Hall Hotel, which had just been erected, one of the largest in the Territory. When Mr. Sinclair came back to Racine he brought with him his family and we took up our residence in one of the only two brick houses in the town.

Before we could adjust ourselves to our new environment we encountered further difficulties. Almost at the outset of our activities in the new field there was a period of "hard times" which, at seemingly regular intervals, occurred to impose further hardship upon the struggling settlers. Business was demoralized and there was little or no market for the products of the farms. The Sinclair family, also, after residing at Racine for five or six weeks, found life there too monotonous after the advantages of Bangor. Mr. Sinclair, therefore, decided to return to Milwaukee, which he did in January, 1846, renting a house on Mason Street.

This gave me another opportunity to resume my interrupted studies for about three months, until April 1, 1846, during which time I went to school at "Professor" Skinner's on what is now Jefferson Street. In the meantime Mr. Sinclair made a trip to Escanaba. He took with him two teams and sleighs laden with supplies for his camps, the first to go northward on the ice on Green Bay. From Milwaukee to Green Bay City the country was to some extent settled but beyond that point it was practically uninhabited except for the Indians, who maintained a small settlement or center at the mouth of the Menominee River on the site of the present city of Marinette, and several small lumbering settlements.

With the advent of spring I set out for Janesville to begin the work of "breaking" some of the land which Mr. Sinclair owned in Rock Prairie, about five miles south of the village and within three miles of Turtleville, or Turtle Creek, as it was then called. There were two sections, twenty-eight and twenty-nine, with smaller parcels near by. I left Milwaukee with a six-horse team, which I drove through Water Street, and a wagon laden with lumber and supplies with which to build a shanty to begin farming operations in April.

We brought two hundred acres under cultivation, one hundred and thirty of which I plowed alone, and paid a neighboring farmer two dollars an acre to cultivate two hundred more. Turning the unbroken soil was no easy task. The plows held themselves, making a furrow twenty-two inches wide and only two and one-half inches deep, but the turf was tough with roots in places and it was necessary to stop and sharpen the share with a file about every mile of the distance traversed. This required some skill, as the share, if not pitched correctly, would cant out of the furrow or bury itself in the ground.

Our equipment, as might be expected, was somewhat primitive. For plowing, oxen were generally used, for which purpose they were better suited in many respects to the conditions then prevailing than horses. They required no water, a decided advantage in view of the fact that we were obliged to haul our supply from Turtle Creek, two miles away. It was not until some time later that we sank a well, being obliged to dig ninety-five feet before

striking the water level. Neither was it necessary to feed
the oxen. They sustained themselves on such provender
as they were able to secure when they were turned out at
night to graze.

We purchased six yoke of oxen, together with a
"hoosier" wagon, a large covered vehicle built in Pennsylvania in 1834, from the Lovejoys, of Princeton, Illinois,
cousins of Mr. Sinclair, who afterwards became persons of
some notoriety. One of them, Owen, was a Congregational
minister with an ambition to go to Congress. I heard
him say to Mr. Sinclair, using the expression of the time:
"Eight dollars a day and roast beef is better than preaching
in a country village." All of them were abolitionists and
gained distinction as orators during the agitation over the
fugitive slave question.

Another of the brothers, Elijah, established a newspaper
in Missouri and became so energetic in his support of the
abolitionist propaganda that a mob one evening descended
upon his newspaper office, seized the printing press and
threw it into the river. Undeterred by this misadventure
he went to Alton, Illinois, and established another paper
devoted to the same cause. He was shot without warning
one evening while standing in the doorway of his office.
Owen Lovejoy achieved his ambition to serve in Congress
in 1858 and was re-elected in 1860. During the following
year, after the outbreak of the war, while delivering a
speech in the House of Representatives he stalked defiantly
down the middle aisle of the chamber and with clenched
fist turned toward the Southern members and said: "You
murdered my brother more than twenty years ago and I
am here to-day to vindicate his blood."

Hard as the work was at the farm at Janesville our
earlier efforts did not meet with success. The first crop

of wheat was killed during the winter. The second crop rusted. At the same time the price was so low, only forty cents a bushel at Milwaukee, that it was scarcely worth the trouble of hauling it from Janesville. In spite of such early failures and the difficulties of breaking a way the tide of development swept on apace. In 1846 and again in 1850 on my way from Janesville to Milwaukee I passed from fifty to one hundred teams within a single mile, all hauling wheat to market. Not infrequently during this period, after the long and arduous task of cultivating the stubborn soil, sowing and harvesting his crop and transporting it to Milwaukee, the farmer received for a load little more than sufficient, after deducting his expenses, to purchase a few boards and a barrel of salt and other supplies.

In many instances the trip from the farm was longer than could be made in a single day and lodging houses were established along the road where, for approximately sixty-two and one-half cents, five "bits," a farmer could secure lodging and two meals for himself and stable room and hay for his horses. Of these institutions one of the most notable along the Janesville road was at East Troy, thirty-one miles west of Milwaukee, conducted by a man named Thayer, a favorite stopping place for teamsters who slept in a large room which, in taverns throughout the West generally, was designated the "school section." Each lodger, if he wished it, was given a cigar and glass of whiskey, both of indifferent quality, night and morning. It was a far cry from these establishments to the taverns along the St. John and the Penobscot stage route but they served the purpose for which they were created very well.

The road from Janesville to Milwaukee was a part of the main route from the lead district in the vicinity of Galena, Illinois, then the most notable town of the northern

Mississippi River region. Farther south, toward Chicago, — a city relatively of much less consequence in the West than it was to become after the advent of the railroads,— the roads were usually in bad condition and at times impassable, a fact which accounted for the more rapid development of Milwaukee at the outset of its history. The lead wagons, largely of the "hoosier" type, were drawn by from five to seven yoke of oxen and the drivers during the journey slept in their wagons at night. On this same route was a stage line, with coaches leaving daily, from Milwaukee to Janesville, a distance of sixty-five miles, conducted by Davis and Moore. Its equipment was much less elaborate than the Concord coaches and well-groomed horses that carried one from Mattawamkeag to Bangor and the drivers were much humbler individuals. They received only twelve dollars a month and performed as well the duties of hostler.

In this environment the knowledge of oxen I had gained in the woods in Maine proved to be of great value to me. Mr. Sinclair, who was of a most practical turn of mind, was desirous of outdoing his friend "Mose" Ryan,— who with his brother, Stover Ryan, whom I have mentioned in connection with the Aroostook War, came from Maine some years before,— in hauling flour and commissioned me to perform that exploit. I had been associated with him long enough to know that whenever he gave an order he expected it to be carried out regardless of the cost or consequences and I acted accordingly. Discarding my clothes, which I put in a paper bag, for a pair of overalls and a "hickory" shirt, the garb most frequently seen on the highway, I hooked up five yoke of cattle in October, 1847, and at Jackman's mill loaded twenty-five barrels of flour. This was the largest load ever hauled over the Janesville road, at least up to that time. Some drivers had taken as much as twenty-two barrels with a team of six horses in the winter time but no one had even approached in the summer the record I had established. Instead of a goad stick I used a whip similar to those with which the lead teamsters were equipped, a fifteen-foot pole with a lash of the same length. Slowly and laboriously we plodded along but we progressed steadily and reached our destination without mishap. These and many other trials of skill and capacity were a part of Mr. Sinclair's method of schooling me to meet the problems of the time and since then I have had many occasions to be grateful for the experience so obtained.

I have not exhausted the catalogue of difficulties which the early settlers of the Middle West encountered. In addition to "hard times," the disastrous cold of the winters, and the drouth of the summers which sometimes withered the crops, there were epidemics of "ague-and-chill fever," malaria, which ran in virulent form through the Middle West. It was a common saying at the time that in Illinois and Indiana even the dogs shook in the spring and autumn and reports of the unwelcome visitation carried back to the East caused many who were contemplating moving to the new country to hesitate, as I had occasion to discover at first hand on my trips to Maine.

In 1846 and again in 1850 most of the people living in the vicinity of the lakes, principally in Manistee, Muskegon, Grand Haven and other places on the lower peninsula of Michigan, in middle and southern Wisconsin and in Illinois and Indiana were afflicted with the disease. It seemed to descend upon the country like a blanket and the popular superstition was that it was due to the plowing of the "wild" soil. Few escaped it and I was no exception to the general rule. For a time I was obliged to abandon my work and put myself into the hands of Dr. Wolcott, one of the best known physicians in Milwaukee. Although I recovered sufficiently to go to Escanaba in the latter part of 1846, the malady was tenacious and I did not rid myself of it entirely for five or six years. During this period I had a recurrence almost every time I went to Chicago or Milwaukee.

On every side one came in contact with the unfortunate victims of the disease, sometimes trembling in the throes of a chill, sometimes burning with a raging fever. It was no marvel that exaggerated reports of the prevalence of the scourge were carried back East. The salutary effect of quinine as a remedy was very little appreciated at this early day. Many still regarded it as a dangerous medicine and in most cases if it were administered at all it was given in such small quantities, in fourthproof brandy, that it was entirely ineffective. I myself took liberal doses of it often by the spoonful, in its unadulterated form, and have relied upon it to a large extent ever since. To its stimulating effect I owe relief from many possible illnesses. The "chills and fever" did not disappear entirely until 1869 or 1870 and the only way of escaping it for a long time seemed to be to go north of Green Bay, beyond which latitude it did not extend in Wisconsin.

It was not my fate, nor was it Mr. Sinclair's purpose, that I devote myself to farming as a career. My training in this branch of activity was concluded with the brief experiences I have narrated. Thereafter my attention was to be absorbed by lumbering with the exception of brief excursions into other fields such as sailing. In 1846 Mr. Sinclair purchased from George Dousman, the "forwarder and warehouse man" of Milwaukee, the schooner

"Nancy Dousman" for use in connection with the mill at Escanaba. The vessel, which I hauled out on the ways, was cut in two and lengthened twenty-five feet, rechristened the "Gallinipper" and placed under command of Captain George W. Ford. In the autumn with a number of other men, among whom was Henry Gunsaulus — the uncle of Dr. Frank Gunsaulus, of Chicago — who was to receive wages of fourteen dollars a month as an axeman and sawyer, we embarked on the vessel for Escanaba or Flat Rock, arriving there on November 5.

At this time the entire region north of the city of Green Bay, formerly an army post, sometimes called Navarino, was practically a wilderness and the northern peninsula of Michigan was a trackless forest, the main outpost being Sault Sainte Marie, where Fort Brady was situated. There were two mills of considerable size at Green Bay, a large mill at the mouth of the Menominee River, mills with one saw at Oconto, Cedar River, and Ford River, and on the White Fish River at the head of Little Bay de Noc, four mills. At Flat Rock, or Escanaba, the Sinclair and Wells Company operated two mills, one about a mile from the mouth of the river, where the plant of the I. Stephenson Company is now, the other about two miles up. These two mills taken together were considered the largest lumbering establishment in the United States west of the Hudson River. The next in size was probably that at Grand Haven, Michigan, and there were smaller mills at Muskegon and Manistee. Although seemingly numerous these mills were primitive structures mechanically and otherwise and their output was very limited. It would be accurate to say, I think, that in 1846 all of the mills on Green Bay represented an investment of less than fifty thousand dollars and could have been purchased for that amount.

At Escanaba there were not more than a dozen houses, in addition to the company's boarding-house, clustered around each mill. Until 1861 there was not a house from the Escanaba to the Ford River, a stretch of ten miles. Building operations on the site of the present city of Escanaba were not begun until 1863 when the Tilden House,— owned jointly by Perry H. Smith, vice-president of the Northwestern Railroad; Dunlap, the superintendent, and the Ludington and Wells Company, successors to Sinclair and Wells,—was erected. Up to this time the place was known as Sand Point. Neither did the city receive its present name until the branch of the Northwestern Railroad from there to Negaunee was built in 1863. The settlement around the mills was known generally as Flat Rock, a literal translation of the Indian name for the river, Scoo-naw-beh, which ran through a flat, shelving geological formation. In casting about for a name for the station and terminus of the road Smith finally evolved Escanaba and so it was christened on the railroad company's maps.

Little was known of the region to the north with the exception of the old Indian trading settlements along Lake Superior in the vicinity of the Apostle Islands and at Sault Sainte Marie where there was an Astor trading house and a Hudson Bay Company store. Marquette had not yet been established. I remember Robert Graveraet, one of the pioneer mining men of the upper peninsula, representing Boston capitalists, saying that he took Peter White, the pioneer resident, there in 1848 and left him behind in his tent. My first visit to the place was made in the winter of 1851–52 on snow shoes, on which occasion the first town meeting was held.

The mining of iron and copper which, with the forests, was to produce almost fabulous wealth, had not yet begun. A year or two earlier government surveyors at work near Negaunee, puzzled for a long time by the unusual variations of their compasses, which sometimes pointed almost south instead of north, found indications of magnetic iron ore; and the discovery of mass copper, chunks of pure copper weighing in some instances several tons, had just aroused the people along the lake to the possibilities of the mining of this very valuable metal. During the following year, 1848, I saw tons of mass copper on the dock at the "Soo" but no one would have predicted at this time the establishment of the great mines which have since made the region one of the most notable copper districts in the world. But the era of development was soon to begin. In the wake of the sinking of the Jackson mine, the first iron mine to be discovered at Negaunee, came many others and the mineral deposits of the region are still largely unexplored.

Escanaba was the southern outpost for the Lake Superior country. During the summer, of course, transportation was carried on by water, but in the winter time when the lakes were closed to navigation the only avenue of communication was north from Green Bay city on the ice to Escanaba and thence up the supply roads we had established along the Escanaba River to our logging camps. Beyond this point was a trail to Marquette through the forest which one traversed on snow shoes. The mail was transported over this route on toboggans drawn, as a rule, by dogs, the trip from Green Bay requiring approximately six days. Most of the carriers were half-breed Indians or French.

When the Northwestern completed its road from Negaunee to Escanaba a line of steamers from the latter point to the city of Green Bay was established and maintained with a daily service until 1872, after which the railroad was extended northward from Green Bay. In 1846 the Sinclair and Wells Company had carried its logging operations about twenty-five miles up the Escanaba River. Gradually we penetrated farther into the forest and the travel to Lake Superior followed the supply roads as our camps were advanced. Eventually we constructed a logging railroad, the Escanaba and Lake Superior, one hundred and eighty-five miles of roadbed and trackage on the main line and lateral branches, over which large quantities of iron ore from the upper peninsula mines are now transported to the big docks at Wells for transshipment on the lakes.

There were few Indians, when I first went to Escanaba, north of the Menominee River, where there was a trading post, and they gave us no trouble. Some Canadians and half-breeds trapped and hunted in the forests and traded in their pelts at the settlements along Lake Superior, but the evidences of human activity were very scant and the brooding silences of the primeval wilderness were rarely disturbed except by the cry of the wild fowl or the call of the beasts. There were some wolves which seldom molested us, deer were plentiful, and in exploring rivers and streams I came upon many haunts of the industrious beaver. In 1852 I purchased more than forty marten skins at Marquette for eight or nine dollars each. Mink pelts were sold at this time for fifty cents. Not many years later, in accordance, very likely, with the whims of fashion, mink became as expensive as marten had been and the latter could be obtained for one-twentieth of what it had cost before.

In many directions throughout this wilderness I made timber cruising expeditions, locating suitable lands which we purchased from the government, in a region which, so far as I knew, had never been tracked by white men except the surveyors. For several months in the year, particularly in the summer time,— during the winter time we were engaged in logging,— I drove my way through the forests on foot carrying a knapsack and compass with an exploring crew. In a period of twelve years at least four were spent in this fashion. Our equipment was as light as possible. We carried no tents, slept under the open sky, frequently were deluged with rain and at times floundered through bogs and morasses. Oftentimes, too, as we made our way through the dense brush, the moisture on the leaves and branches saturated our garments so that for days at a time, neither awake nor asleep, did we enjoy the comfort of dry clothing. We slept on the ground with a single blanket for covering and at times, after a torrential rain during the night, I awoke at dawn to find that I was lying in a pool of water.

These exploring trips carried me far beyond the range of the known country. In 1850 I went through to the mouth of the Sturgeon River, now Nahma, on Big Bay de Noc, Garden Bay and Fish Dam River at the head of the bay. On the Escanaba River I was the first lumberman to penetrate as far as Cataract Falls, four miles above what is now known as the Princeton mine.

CHAPTER VI

Early lumbering methods in vogue along Green Bay — Invasion of the Maine lumbermen — Introduction of sawed shingles — Marketing lumber at Chicago and Milwaukee — Masting on the Great Lakes — Life in the logging camps — Tea drinking — Log driving on the Escanaba — Locating timber lands — Offering of public lands for sale in 1848 — Trip to the "Soo" — First entry of pine lands on the Menominee River — Meager returns for lumbering.

THE methods of lumber manufacturing in vogue at this time in the pine districts along Green Bay in Wisconsin and Michigan were crude compared to the elaborate system which has since been perfected. The mills, during the decade between 1840 and 1850, were small establishments operated by water power, making approximately one million feet of lumber a year. The type of saw known as the "mulay" had just come in and not a few of the mills were still equipped with the old-fashioned sash saws. The circular saw and the band saw, together with most of the mechanical apparatus now in use for handling logs, had not then been perfected.

In logging, driving and sawing the lumbermen of Maine and New Brunswick were the most expert of their time, and it was largely under their direction and through the introduction of the methods which prevailed along the St. John and Penobscot rivers that lumbering in Wisconsin and on the northern peninsula of Michigan, of the West generally, was brought to the point of its greatest development.

In this respect the firm of Sinclair and Wells enjoyed a decided advantage over their competitors. As I have said Mr. Sinclair was probably the greatest practical lumberman in the country and had not only acquired a large experience but had directed operations of magnitude in Maine. In addition he had brought to Wisconsin men who were schooled in lumbering methods in the Pine Tree State. Among them were David Langley, who came west with us in 1845; Silas Howard, who went on foot from Milwaukee to Flat Rock the same year, and others. For some time afterward his forces were constantly being recruited from Maine. Some of the men I brought out with me when I returned from my trips to the East. When the forests in this territory were cut and opportunities for employment became restricted, thousands of the men who had grown up in them went still farther West to the Pacific coast where they are at work to-day. In this way has the enterprise of Maine exerted a marked influence upon the entire lumber industry of the United States.

It was not long before members of my own family, attracted by the prospects which I unfolded in my letters to them, decided to follow in my footsteps. Two of my brothers, Robert and Samuel, came to Escanaba from their home in Maine in 1849 but remained for only one winter. Perhaps they regarded my enthusiasm over the growing West as unfounded. In June, 1852, however, they made a second venture and this time remained permanently. Both of them took up logging by contract near Masonville, Michigan, and afterward occupied conspicuous places in the lumbering industry on the Menominee River, whither I had preceded them, taking charge of and becoming the owners of some of the important mills on the river at that time.

About 1850 the moving stream from the eastern pineries
to the West attained large proportions, the result, very
largely, of a business depression which left many of the
lumbermen in the older region without occupation. Many
also were attracted to the newer field by Mr. Sinclair, and
following their example still more responded to the growing demand for experienced men. There were no less than
thirty of them one winter at Escanaba who had been camp
"bosses" or logging contractors in Maine.

These men were very different from the workmen of
the present day, a fact due to some extent, possibly, to
the environment in which they lived. In the absence of a
highly organized system of industrial interchange they were
obliged to depend upon their own resources to supply their
needs and their capacity for doing things was developed
accordingly. They could erect camps, make axe handles
and sleighs and many of them were blacksmiths, sawyers
and carpenters capable of undertaking almost any variety
of work. Two-thirds of the men in logging crews I have had
could do these things and, in addition, were excellent
boatmen. At present in a crew of fifty men there is rarely
one man who can do any of them, even the "boss" himself. To supply the deficiency it is necessary to send a
blacksmith and a mechanic into the woods and the axe helves
and other tools are made in factories and included in the
list of supplies. It is said, in explanation, that it is cheaper
to buy articles of this sort than to make them. But they
cost us very little sacrifice of time as we did most of these
tasks at night or on Sundays. The same rule of conduct
applied to the women in the mill settlements who devoted
their evenings and spare moments to knitting instead
of occupying themselves with the diversions of the present
day which were, as a matter of fact, unknown.

Similarly my practical education covered a wide range. I could build a bateau, make all of the tools used for river driving, ox yokes and sleighs, shoe oxen and horses and exercise generally the functions of a blacksmith, carpenter or millwright,—all of which stood me in very good stead.

While other mills along Green Bay were being operated to their full capacity to produce a million feet of lumber a year we were turning out from eight to ten millions besides laths, pickets, and other products. We were also the forerunners in this region in the manufacture of sawed shingles. At this time only shaved shingles were known in the West. About one-third of all the boats plying between the pineries of Wisconsin and Michigan and southern lake ports carried bolts, about four feet long, which were made into shingles by the old process of shaving in the yards at Chicago and Milwaukee, at each of which places probably one hundred men were employed in the work.

Not long after my arrival at Escanaba we added to our mill equipment two shingle machines obtained in Maine, each with a capacity of eight thousand in ten hours. The economy of this method of manufacture was obvious but in the beginning there was a prejudice against sawed shingles in the West and the demand was confined to people who had migrated from the New England States. After a time this was overcome, the older method was abandoned and other mills followed our example. With added improvements in the machines some of the mills produced later from forty to fifty thousand shingles a day.

Milwaukee and Chicago were the chief markets for the Green Bay region and the distributing points whence the lumber was shipped to points in the growing Middle West. In these cities practically all of the mills maintained their own yards, to which the lumber was shipped without drying as soon as made. Mr. Sinclair and his partner, Daniel Wells, owned at this time an interest in the firm of N. Ludington and Company, which maintained yards at both places, and a few years later the Ludingtons, Harrison and Nelson, purchased an interest in and subsequently control of the property at Flat Rock. With the building of railroads and the reduction of freight rates most of the lumber producers abandoned the practice of maintaining their own yards and piled and dried the lumber at the mills shipping it to all points by rail as well as by boat.

For a year or two after the extension of the railroads through the Green Bay region, freight rates were so exorbitant, twelve cents per hundredweight, that there was little change in the methods of transporting of lumber. The railroad officials were brought to the realization of the short-sightedness of their policy by the establishment of a car ferry which ran between Chicago and Peshtigo, connecting at the latter place with a short railroad line, the Wisconsin and Michigan, which ran for some distance up the Menominee River. The loaded cars were transferred to the ferry at Peshtigo and taken thence to Chicago. We were so successful in this method of transportation that the Northwestern and the Chicago, Milwaukee and St. Paul railroads reduced the freight rate from twelve to six and one-half or seven cents. When this was done the Chicago and Milwaukee lumber yards were abandoned and shipments were made direct from the mills.

In 1846, when I first went into the woods at Escanaba, I was able to apply to good purpose the training I had acquired as a boy in the logging camps "down East." The firm of Sinclair and Wells began at that time the production of masts in which trade they had practically a monopoly on the upper lakes. Other lumbermen had the same opportunity but were not skilled in the driving of oxen except in single teams and, consequently, could not haul out of the forest logs of the size and length required for masts and spars. To do this the six-ox team was necessary. The masts were transported in the rough to Chicago and Milwaukee, lashed to the sides of the ships, being too long to be taken aboard, and were finished at the ship yards.

This was the first branch of lumbering I took up in the West. During the winter of 1846 I drove a six-ox team at Escanaba and hauled out of the woods one hundred and fifty masts. It was not such a far cry, after all, from masting on the Great Lakes to the pre-revolutionary period when the English government reserved to itself for the royal navy and marked with broad arrows the tall pines in the forests skirting the St. John River.

Trees of this kind along the lakes are no more. They vanished when the forests were stripped of the white pine, and their lesser brethren, the Norway pine and hardwoods, are following fast after them. In 1846 I hauled from the forest a white pine twelve inches thick at the butt, six inches at the top and one hundred and seven feet long. It was shipped to the yard at Milwaukee where it was made into a "liberty pole" or flagstaff and presented to Rock County. Because of its great length it could not be hauled intact over the crooked roads and had to be sawed in two and spliced. It was erected in the court house yard at Janesville and stood there for many years until it rotted down.

During the winters of 1846, 1847, and 1848 most of my time was devoted to the driving of oxen with a goad stick, after the Yankee fashion, logging along the Escanaba River. This branch of the industry I have always considered the most important. In sawing, which is entirely a matter of mechanical equipment and arrangement, conditions are everywhere equal and no mill enjoys an advantage over competing mills, but in logging there is a wider field for the expenditure of individual effort and the exercise of skill and it is in this that the profits are made or losses of operation sustained. The difference between success and failure oftentimes depends upon the ingenuity displayed in the harvesting of the timber, so to speak, and bringing it to the mills.

Logging conditions were similar to those which prevailed in Aroostook County and in New Brunswick. At the camps, then about twenty-five miles up the Escanaba, we were up for breakfast at five o'clock and off to work before daylight and did not return until dark. By comparison with the supply lists of the logging camps of the present the rations upon which we thrived were, to say the least, meager, and there was not enough variety to tempt even a normal appetite. As there were no farms in the vicinity to rely upon, the supply of vegetables was small. We were rarely able to obtain any at all. For five and one-half months during one winter we did not see a vegetable and were given fresh meat only once. Camp fare consisted of the inevitable pork and beans, bread, and tea which we sweetened with Porto Rico molasses in lieu of sugar. Occasionally we had a little butter and dried apples but so infrequently that they seemed a luxury beyond the conception of even the lumbermen of the present day who have varied camp supply lists to draw upon for subsistence.

For breakfast and supper the beverage was tea, for dinner, only water. Sometimes when I was detained, arriving late at the mess table, I found the water which had been poured into my tin cup frozen and had to break the ice to drink. Tea seemed so much of a luxury that I promised myself that, if I ever had a home of my own and was able to afford myself that enjoyment, I would have tea three times a day. For almost seventy years I have adhered to that resolution. It happened afterwards that Potter Palmer, of Chicago, and I became very good friends and, whether by reason of his earlier experiences or not, he seemed to regard tea-drinking in much the same light as myself. For a number of years he obtained his supply from Sir Thomas Lipton, whom I had met with him in Chicago, and he shared it with me.

Sunday, as in the East also, was a day of rest, the kind of rest that takes the form of a change of occupation. The men in charge of the camps made axe handles, filed saws and ground axes. Despite all these apparent hardships, the long hours, the hazardous nature of the work, and the lack of luxuries we did well enough. Our work was such that we needed no special stimulus to whet our appetites. We made the most of our unvarying fare and ate with a zest that comes only of long days of work in the open, the keen, crisp air of the winter and the tang of the pine forests.

In late years the methods of logging have been entirely modified. More men are employed to do the same amount of work and the cost has become proportionately greater. As the forests along the streams were cleared and the hard wood, which cannot be floated, came into demand, the tree trunks were cut into short lengths in the forest, hauled to the railroad on sleighs drawn in some cases by steam tractors and transported to the mills overland. In this way the dangers of log driving have been obviated and time economized to a moderate degree, but the much-heralded progress in the promotion of efficiency of labor has not, so far as I can see, wrought any improvement upon the logging methods we followed sixty-five years ago. Then the foremen worked as leaders rather than directors. In the woods and working rollways or jams they took the initiative and set the example for the men, the only effective way, to my mind, to handle them under such conditions. Nowadays the system used on the railroads is followed,—the foreman looks on and gives orders. If his attention is diverted the men work indifferently or not at all until they are again under observation.

Many of those who worked in the lumber camps and at the mills in Wisconsin and Michigan were Germans who made their way westward in great numbers. They were not very efficient as water men or for log driving, but steadier than the laborers of any other nationality. Whether or not the watchful eye of the "boss" was on them they kept to their tasks with unflagging energy. I found generally that the men needed no close supervision. At Marinette, when I first took charge of the mill of the N. Ludington Company, as part owner and manager, they made it a point to cut more lumber, if possible, when I was away in attendance upon the meeting of the county board or elsewhere, than when I was present.

During the spring of 1847 I went on the drive down the Escanaba River. This work, done by the men who had been engaged in cutting timber during the winter, was more or less dangerous. The stream was shallow and swift of current and its course lies through a country underlaid with a ledge of flat rock. To avoid having the logs swept away by the ice freshets, which sometimes came down with great force, it was necessary for us to pile them on rollways on the banks whence they were turned into the water when the danger had passed. Following the

custom that had prevailed in Maine the logs were barked
when hauled from the forest, and when the rollways were
broken out they rushed with dangerous momentum down
the banks into the river.

Because of the flat shores it was necessary for us oftentimes to work waist deep in the icy water to keep the stream
of logs moving. In April, 1848, when the winter was
scarcely over and the weather still cold, we met with these
conditions and I suggested to two of my men,— William
Phelps, who came from New York, and an Irishman named
Barney Gurtie,— that we go into the water. Gurtie,
who was somewhat older than Phelps and myself, remained
for two hours, at the end of which time the ice was forming
on our handspikes and clothing.   Phelps and I kept at the
task for four hours although our flesh was blue and our
teeth chattering as if we had the ague. From such exposure we suffered no ill whatever.

Although the conditions we encountered in driving
and sacking logs were uncomfortable my crews lost less
time than in the camps in winter. Sometimes the men
injured their feet in log jams but otherwise they were in
better physical condition; and subjecting them to hardships
which, from the latter day point of view, might have been
considered inhumane, seemed to do them more good than
harm. They worked cheerfully, at least, on wages of from
twelve to fifteen dollars a month and seemed to accomplish
more than men who are now paid two dollars and a half a
day.

One of the most important aspects of the lumbering
industry during the period from 1845 to 1860 was "exploring" or "cruising," the location of timber in the little
known stretch of forest. In the forties the government
was making a survey of the lands in the upper peninsula of

Michigan. The work was originally undertaken by Dr. Houghton, who lost his life in the wilderness, and William Burt and was being continued by the sons of the latter. "Judge" Burt was the inventor of the solar compass, which obviated the difficulties that had been encountered with the magnetic compass by reason of the deflection due to the presence of magnetic iron ore in the region. He received a premium for it from the government and several efforts were made to induce Congress to pass a bill paying him further compensation for the use of the instrument.

To the study of surveying, as it was adapted to the needs of the lumberman, I gave much attention and acquired some proficiency in tracing and locating timber, exploring the forest for advantageously situated pine, and outlining it on the maps so that it could be entered for purchase. The first of the land north of the Straits of Mackinac was offered for public sale by the government in July, 1848. To take early advantage of the opportunity Mr. Sinclair and I left Milwaukee, where I was at the time, during July, for Sault Sainte Marie where the land office had been established in one of the old Fort Brady buildings.

We went on the steamer "Nile,"— one of the vessels of the line owned by Mr. Newberry, of Detroit, which ran between Chicago and Buffalo,—as far as Mackinac, and there boarded a smaller steamer, the "Ben Franklin," commanded by a Captain Jones. We arrived at our destination about a week before the beginning of the sale. Three days later we were joined by Mr. Sinclair's partner, Daniel Wells, who had done some government surveying in Florida in 1832 and was skilled in this sort of work.

Such latter day conveniences as mapping paper, blotting paper, mucilage and envelopes were not obtainable, but with the materials at hand Mr. Wells made several tracings from the government maps inserting free handed the rivers, swamps, and lakes.   For $1.25 an acre, the minimum price for public lands, we bid in areas at the mouths of the Escanaba River, Ford River, and Sturgeon River, now Nahma, and also an island on which the chemical works and furnaces at Gladstone, Michigan, now stand.

For five or six years after this opening sale I went to the "Soo" three or four times a year to enter lands for the Sinclair and Wells Company and, in conjunction with my forest explorations, acquired a very thorough knowledge of lands in the northern peninsula.   Later my activities took me southward along the Green Bay and in August and September, 1853, I took a crew of men, among them two of my brothers and William Holmes, now of Menominee, Michigan, to the land office at Manasha, Wisconsin, to make the first entry of pine land on the Menominee River.   On some of this I am cutting timber even at the present day, the last remnant of the pine forests remaining on the river which only thirty years ago was the greatest timber producing region in America.   Some of it, also, after more than a half century, stripped of timber, is selling as farming land for many times the original price paid for it and the green fields are gradually obliterating the blackened stumps, all that are left of the great forests that stretched away on all sides when I first set foot in them.

In retrospect much has been written of the great wealth these vanished forests have yielded, highly colored narratives of the beginning, growth and decay of the lumbering industry from the point of view of those who have seen little more than the results and nothing at all of the processes.   In reckoning the billions of feet that have

Daniel Wells Jr

been cut, the vanishing of the wilderness and the magical
appearance of the fertile farms, many historians overlook the hardships that were encountered, the difficulties
with which the path of progress was strewn. Nor is sufficient consideration given the good that was achieved,—
the upbuilding of the great prairie states into which the
flood of immigration poured.

In the days when I began my career on the Escanaba
River, lumber was sold for six and eight dollars a thousand
feet. The same grade of lumber in the present market
would be worth from twenty-five to thirty dollars. The
meager returns were scarcely worth the struggle of blazing
a way into the forest and risking the dangers that confronted the pioneer. Where some succeeded many failed,
and if the opportunities of the time were contemplated
face to face and not through the perspective of more than
a half century I doubt very much whether many of the
present generation could have been induced to take their
chances confronted by such disconcerting odds.

CHAPTER VII

The problem of transporting lumber — Great Lakes neglected by
federal government — Dangerous voyages — Inaccessibility of
Green Bay region — Experiences as a sailor before the mast —
I ship as mate — I purchase interest in schooner Cleopatra and
become captain — Development of shipping on the lakes — Early
trips up Green Bay rivers — Introduction of tugs.

THE problem of transportation was almost as important to the lumber industry as the problem of production itself. The era of railroads had not yet begun and the isolated mills at the mouths of the rivers emptying into Green Bay, Big Bay de Noc, and Bay de Noquette,— practically the entire northern lake region,— depended upon boats to bring them supplies and to take their output to market.

The importance of navigation on the lakes, although it was the great highway between the East and West over which the grain from the rapidly growing prairie states was carried in exchange for the manufactured products of the older cities along the seaboard, was not generally recognized by the federal government. The harbors were in wretched condition and lights and buoys to guide the mariner and warn him of dangerous passages were few.

When I came west in 1845 there was only nine feet of water in Milwaukee harbor and conditions at Chicago were just as bad. Neither were there any tugs to assist a vessel to a safe berth. In Chicago, for many years, ships were pulled out of the river to the lake by hand, a head wind necessitating the use of a windlass. What little aid had been extended by the federal government in improving these conditions was withdrawn in 1842 or 1843 when the Democratic administration, then in power, suspended all appropriations for river and harbor work. As a result every sailor on the lakes became a Whig and afterwards a Republican.

The idea that the lakes were little more than a "goose pond" prevailed in Congress for some years later. I remember hearing Captain Blake, a veteran of the battle of Lake Erie, who had achieved notoriety in these waters in the early days for his profanity and red waistcoats, expressing the fervent hope, when he had a United States Senator aboard as a passenger, that he might run into a gale to convince the unsuspecting legislator of the hazards of inland navigation. Even at the "Soo," the great gateway from Lake Superior, no improvements had been made and freight was transferred around the rapids on a small tramway.

Sailing a ship was not unlike blazing a way through the forest. With conditions wretched as they were the navigator was practically without charts and the master figured his course as nearly as he could, estimating the leeway and varying influence of the winds. By comparison with the difficulties that confronted us the lot of the sailors of the present day is an easy one. With compasses and lights the course of their vessels is as plain as the tracks of a railroad, and the steam-driven propellers keep the ship to it without variation and bring her to harbors equipped with all the aids modern ingenuity has been able to devise.

Among the trips we made in the forties was one, which I still have vividly in mind, from Racine to Escanaba on a vessel laden with hay for the lumber camps. After setting sail we saw neither light nor land but followed our un-

charted course very much as instinct guided us. Through
Death's Door, the narrow passage from Lake Michigan
into Green Bay, we groped, feeling our way with the lead
line, and headed cautiously for the mouth of the Flat
Rock or Escanaba River. Proceeding blindly, sounding
as we went, we came about in five feet of water, stirring up
sawdust from one of the mills. From this position we
retreated cautiously to deeper water, lowered a boat,
pulled ashore in the dense fog and with the aid of a compass
found our general bearings. I returned to the ship and
when the fog lifted detected a vessel lying close by. To
our intense relief we discovered that we were in the right
anchorage.

At no time during these early voyages did it seem that
we were free from threatened danger. The officers were
constantly on the alert. During these years I made several
trips with Captain Davis, of the "Champion," as a passenger.
While the boat was under way he never took off his clothes
so that he might be prepared to answer a call to the deck
at any moment.

To make our situation worse the Green Bay region
was largely inaccessible, except through the dangerous
passage, Death's Door, and a long detour was necessary
to clear the peninsula. This disadvantage was overcome
to some extent later by the construction of the Sturgeon
Bay Canal. At the mills also, where there were no harbor
facilities, loading the vessels was difficult as they were
anchored some distance off shore and the cargoes had to be
taken out in scows or rafts. Gradually we improved these
conditions and the problem was eventually solved by the
construction of harbors and the building of railroads.

As I have said I had already had a glimpse of the sea
at St. John, New Brunswick, and at Boston and Bangor,

and was on the verge of embarking on Captain Eustis's ship for Nova Scotia as a cabin boy when fate stepped in and decreed otherwise. No one could have lived in Maine during the early part of the last century without having given ear in some measure to the call of the sea. Nearly half the people of New England were sailors when I was a youth, a condition which maintained for the United States an enviable position as a maritime power and led to the upbuilding of a great merchant marine before the Civil War. Whaling, too, was a great industry. Many of the men who attended Harvard and other universities went on a whaling voyage for two or three years before taking up their professions or, possibly, for lack of opportunities to take them up, or sailed for a time before the mast. One of these, a Harvard graduate, I came in contact with on a trip from Milwaukee to Escanaba. As a common seaman he received wages of sixteen dollars a month.

At Bangor, when I was a youth and the spell of the sea was upon me, I had laid awake many nights and in the calm security of my bed pictured myself as the master of a vessel on the lee shore in a gale of wind. The small catalogue of nautical terms at my command I used with extraordinary facility and issued orders with decisiveness and despatch. In these imaginative predicaments I never lost a ship.

My interest in seamanship was revived by my experiences on the lakes which had an element of danger sufficient to stimulate a young man's passion for adventure and the time came when I wanted to try sailing as a reality. Frequently in the summer time I was a passenger on the vessels on which we transported lumber from Escanaba to Milwaukee. On more than one occasion I was permitted to take the wheel. Besides, at Escanaba on Sundays, the only time I had to myself, I availed myself of every opportunity to practice sailing and became so proficient that as early as 1848 I had acquired something of a reputation as a sailor.

At this period the Mackinaw boat was the most common type of small vessel in use and was deemed the most effective for all sorts of weather. They were particularly seaworthy and, if properly handled, could survive any gale on the lakes. These and sailing vessels carrying both passengers and freight were the only means of transportation we had on Green Bay and between Green Bay points and Milwaukee and Chicago during the navigating season from April 1st to November 30th. During the remainder of the year the bay was frozen and to communicate with Green Bay city we went on the ice. I also had opportunity to exercise my ingenuity in sailing a Mackinaw boat at the "Soo," where I went to enter lands for the company. Louis Dickens, one of the pioneer merchants, was always willing to turn over his vessel to me and I made numerous short excursions in the waters in the vicinity. Several years later, in 1858, I brought to Marinette a very good Mackinaw boat which, in a heavy sea, I ran over the bar into the Menominee River.

My desire to sail before the mast had always met with the unrelenting opposition of Mr. Sinclair and, as a result of his maneuvering, my experiences in that direction were confined to a single trip. He evidently proceeded upon the theory that an unlimited dose of sailing would cure me of any weakness I had for the sea, or the lakes, as it happened to be, and he took occasion to administer it on a trip from Milwaukee to Escanaba and return on the large schooner "Champion."

The owner of the vessel was Mr. George Dousman who, as I have said before, was engaged in the shipping and warehouse business in Milwaukee. He was a friend of Mr. Sinclair, and by his direction — the conspiracy having been arranged beforehand— Captain Davis, the commander of the "Champion," made it a point to show me no favors on this my first voyage as a real sailor and to accord me no more consideration than was given the other men. When we left Milwaukee I went into the forecastle with the crew and performed the duties allotted to me. We reached Escanaba without mishap, took on a cargo of lumber and returned to Milwaukee.

Mr. Sinclair, by accident or design, was a passenger on the return trip. Having doubtless kept me under scrutiny and thinking that his plan had succeeded by this time, he asked me one morning where I had slept.

"In the forecastle with the men," I replied.

"Didn't you feel mean with a lot of drunken sailors?" he added.

"No," I said. "Here in the vessel I am a sailor before the mast as they are and I can't prevent their drinking."

Perhaps I was somewhat defiant but, to myself, I was ready to admit that I had my fill of sailing, at least as an occupant of the forecastle. None the less I completed the voyage. When we arrived at Milwaukee and the men prepared to unload the boat, which was the custom at that time, I needed no further discouragement and told Captain Davis that he might put a man in my place. I kept my own counsel but I had made up my mind that sailing was not a desirable avocation and that the wages of sixteen dollars a month during the summer and from twenty to twenty-six dollars on the last trip in the fall were very small compensation for the hard work and discomforts to which one was subjected.

Later Mr. Sinclair talked to me about my lost aspirations in a more kindly vein and advised me not to choose a career of this kind. When he asked me to get into the carriage and go with his family to Janesville, I went without urging, but I made no confession of defeat, keeping that part of the situation to myself.

This experience was the extent of my career as an ordinary seaman but I had not yet done with sailing. A short time after going to the farm Mr. Sinclair sent me to the "Soo" to enter lands while he went to the mills at Escanaba. There he purchased the schooner "Gallinipper" — the boat which I had hauled out on the ways several years before — and instructed me to hire Captain Johnson Henderson, or anyone else I might select, to take command of her. I made the arrangement with Henderson, who carried lumber from Escanaba for two or three years, until he lost the vessel, and went with him as mate.

The first few trips were uneventful but in the early part of September, 1850, while on our way to Escanaba, with the boat light, we ran into a storm. There were eight passengers aboard, a yawl in tow and a horse on deck all bound for Bailey's Harbor. The yawl could not be taken aboard because the schooner was very "crank" when unladen and had capsized two years before at Presque Isle on Lake Huron.

A terrific gale came up and, while fighting the storm from Friday morning to Sunday afternoon, we drifted from what is now called Algoma, then known as Wolf River, twelve miles south of Sturgeon Bay, to a point ten miles south of Racine. The yawl parted its painter and went adrift to the east side of the lake; the horse died at midnight on Sunday when we were off Milwaukee harbor, and the passengers, who had despaired of ever seeing land again, were back where they had started. The storm which we had happily survived was said to be one of the most severe that ever swept Lake Michigan. At Milwaukee just as we were about to embark upon the momentous voyage I had met a Captain Davis, the owner of a vessel called the "General Thornton," who was preparing to cross the lake for Manistee where he was to take on a cargo. He also ran into the storm, his ship went down and all of the crew were drowned. He saved his own life by lashing himself to a spar on which he floated for six days and eleven hours before he was picked up. Famished and exhausted he sought to keep himself alive by sucking the blood from his arm. A number of years later some of the old lake captains wrote to me asking for information concerning Captain Davis, who was a Welshman and an interesting character, but I knew nothing of him except that he had gone to Chicago where he was employed in a sail loft. After that I had lost trace of him.

After I had made a few trips on the "Gallinipper" as mate the company commissioned me to buy horses, oxen and supplies, another ruse of Mr. Sinclair's to divert my attention from sailing. Mrs. Sinclair, whose maternal interest in me had not diminished, also pleaded with me to give it up as a career. None the less I was still absorbed in it and during the following year, 1851, I purchased a half interest in the "Gallinipper" on July 5, when she was on her way to Escanaba. This was not a fortunate venture. On July 7, when off Sheboygan the vessel capsized and sank, a total loss although all of the crew were saved. The transaction not having been recorded with the underwriters I saved my outlay for the purchase. The untoward experience did not deter me from making further ventures of the same kind. Shortly afterward I went to Milwaukee and bought the controlling half interest in the schooner "Cleopatra" from Captain William Porter. The ship was under charter, the Sinclair and Wells Company owning one half. I came in on her to Escanaba and about sunrise went ashore to make arrangements for taking on a load of lumber. Mr. Sinclair was just sitting down to breakfast.

"Where did you come from?" he asked in surprise.

"Milwaukee," I replied.

"On what vessel?"

"The 'Cleopatra'."

"Did you buy Captain Porter out?" he asked, evidently suspecting what had happened.

"Yes," I said.

"Who is captain of the vessel now?"

"They call me captain when I am aboard," I replied.

This brief interchange obviously convinced Mr. Sinclair, who was a man of much determination, that I had taken up sailing in earnest and he capitulated, making no further effort to dissuade me from my course. "Sit down," he said, "and eat your breakfast." That ended the episode.

I made nine trips on the "Cleopatra" during the summer and autumn of 1851, and netted in profits six hundred dollars. Freight rates, however, were low and the returns small compensation for the outlay and the hard work, not to speak of the risk encountered. The following year I made only one trip, after which I put another man in my place and went back East and was married. I had definitely and finally arrived at the conclusion that sailing was too hazardous an occupation and offered no attractions as a permanent career. In 1853 I sold my interest in the vessel, deciding that I wanted no more of it as seaman, officer or vessel owner.

Although I had abandoned this course the experience I had on the water was none the less valuable, and I never lost interest in this phase of activity on the lakes. The development of water transportation, particularly in connection with the commercial growth of Wisconsin and Michigan, is a fascinating story, especially to one such as I who has seen the sailing vessels and side-wheelers of the mid-century give way to the great freighters plying between the commercial centers which once seemed mere villages on the fringe of a vast wilderness. The outlines of the earlier period are growing dimmer as they recede with the years, but I am not likely to forget, however little it may interest later generations, that to the men who then sailed the lakes are due the honors of pioneering no less than the men who brought the unbroken prairie to bear and laid open the wealth of the forests.

In some of the less important nautical incidents of this time I played a small part. The first steamboat that came into the Escanaba River was the "Trowbridge," a small side-wheeler, built in Milwaukee and used to carry passengers ashore from the Buffalo boats. In 1845 the vessel carried an excursion party to Green Bay and ran into the Escanaba to obtain wood sufficient to carry it back to Milwaukee or Washington Harbor, the latter a place frequented by steamers on the route from Buffalo to Green Bay. The next steamer to enter the Escanaba was the "Queen City," a vessel drawing only forty inches, which I took up as far as the water-mills in 1858. Isolated as we were, excursions of this kind were about the only diversion to which we had recourse on days of leisure, and women and children as well as the men were only too glad to avail themselves of an opportunity to take a trip of this kind. A number of times I commandeered all the vessels at hand on which practically the entire population of the small settlements embarked for an outing.

The "Morgan L. Martin," a Fox River boat, was the first vessel on the Menominee River to tow scows and rafts of lumber from the mills to vessels at anchor outside the bar. At this time, 1860, the Menominee had no harbor improvements, and there was only from three and one-half to four feet of water at the mouth. It was the practice of the mill owners to pull the scows and rafts out to the waiting vessels by hand, a process which cost from five to ten dollars, low as wages were at the time. Not long after I took charge of the mill of the N. Ludington Company at Marinette, we decided to experiment with a tug and purchased the "Morgan L. Martin" with this end in view. In this we were successful. We found that we could reduce the cost of towing more than one-half. During the first year we charged $1.50 to tow a scow both ways. The next year the price was increased to $2.00. The mill owners, who looked upon the experiment with scepticism, soon came to the conclusion that the tug was indispensable, and we added two or three more to our equipment.

The "Morgan L. Martin" was of so light a draft, thirty inches, that it could venture into streams which were not considered navigable for steam vessels. I took her into Cedar River for the first trip that had ever been made by a boat of her type in that region, and into Ford River where the water was very shallow. But the most unusual achievement of the vessel was a trip four miles up the White Fish River to the water-mill, which I took in 1860 with one hundred and fifty people from Flat Rock and Masonville, one Sunday afternoon. This was hailed as an extraordinary nautical event, the first and probably the only occasion when a vessel of considerable size had gone so far up the river. As we threaded our way cautiously up the narrow stream the echo of our whistle reached the ears of Peter Murphy, the superintendent of the White Fish property, who was in one of the waterwheel pits making repairs. When we neared the mill he emerged covered with grease and astonished beyond measure at the unfamiliar sight. For a time, he said, he was almost convinced that the boat was approaching overland from Lake Superior on the Grand Island trail. In celebration of the event he wished to serve dinner for the entire party, but I persuaded him instead to accompany us in his boat back to Masonville. When we came to turn about we found it necessary to shovel away a portion of the river bank to give us adequate space and Burleigh Perkins, one of the pioneers of the region, and some other men edged the steamer around with handspikes.

CHAPTER VIII

IN the meantime the opportunities for lumbering broadened. The Middle West was in the full swing of development. Farms were multiplying and cities and towns were adding to their population by leaps and bounds. On the one side was the expanding market; on the other the pine forests. The need of the moment was for practical lumbermen who knew how to meet the problems presented by logging, manufacturing and transportation, the connecting links between the supply and demand.

The greatest difficulty arose from the lack of men capable of taking charge of and directing these operations. In most instances those who had established mills knew little or nothing of lumbering itself, and it was not long before many found themselves involved in complications from which they could not unaided extricate themselves. At the same time the West supplied few men who had been schooled in the forest. To obtain them it was necessary to go back to the older communities in Maine and New Brunswick, and the lumbermen from this territory in increasing numbers migrated to the forests of Wisconsin,

Michigan, and Minnesota, where afterward many of them attained positions of independence in the rapidly growing settlements.

With Mr. Sinclair behind me and opportunity ahead, my advancement toward a position of independence was fairly rapid and it was not long before I began to reap the benefits of my arduous training. In the winters of 1846, 1847, and 1848 I had been occupied chiefly with hauling logs out of the woods to the mills at Flat Rock, driving teams of six oxen with a goad stick in the Yankee fashion. On November 22, 1848, when I was nineteen years old, I moved a step upward in the scale, taking charge of logging operations for Sinclair and Wells.

With my crew and horses I went up the Escanaba River ten miles and established my first camp. The winter was severe. The snow was from four to four and one-half feet deep, and we existed as in a state of siege with the white barrier drawn close about us, isolated from the outer world except for the supply road to the mill at the mouth of the river. Under such conditions, I discovered, heavy responsibilities rested upon the camp "boss." Recalcitrants had to be punished summarily, which required a strong arm and a heavy fist, as they could not be turned out upon a snowbound wilderness. Primitive methods of maintaining discipline, however, worked no harm. Many of the men who were subjected to them not only became excellent workmen but also had the good grace to admit afterward that the effects were most salutary and opened their eyes to their own shortcomings.

With my men at this first camp I had very little trouble. Two-thirds of them were Germans who worked willingly and well and were not given to dissension. During this year, also, the first of the Scandinavians,— Norwegians and

Swedes,—who were to settle large areas in northern Wisconsin and Minnesota arrived. Among the Germans I was fortunate in having one, a recent immigrant, "Barney" Nicholas by name, who took naturally to the driving of oxen. Under my tutelage he soon learned to take two or three trees to a load, after I had hauled them from the stump to the main road, and within a month could make the trip to the rollway without assistance. I have never seen him from that day to this but have been told that in later years he lived somewhere between West Bend and Fond du Lac and had accumulated a small fortune, which he undoubtedly deserved.

In the winter of 1850–1851 I arrived at the point of independence and entered into contracts with Sinclair and Wells to put in logs at a fixed price per thousand feet. This, as I have said, was no mean labor but to me it brought very satisfactory results. I was able to lay by some additions to my small capital and was so well satisfied with the progress I had made that I continued logging under the same conditions for three years, purchasing more teams and equipment and hiring more men.

At the same time other opportunities were held out to me from almost every lumbering establishment in the northern Green Bay region, where mill owners unaccustomed to the wilderness were floundering in the maze of problems it presented. One of these was a Mr. Billings, who had constructed a mill at Ford River, near Escanaba. This property represented a considerable outlay from the point of view of that time. It consisted, in addition to the mill, of a village, store, lumbering outfit, twelve yoke of cattle and six pairs of horses. There were a million feet of very good logs in the pond, a million feet of lumber at the mill, sixty men at work in the woods, and supplies sufficient for

Water Mill on the Escanaba River built in 1844

the winter. In the autumn of 1850 Mr. Billings volunteered to give me a deed to half these possessions on condition that I go to Ford River and manage the property while
he made a visit to his old home in Massachusetts. To insure
my having full control of operations he agreed to remain
away for two years, leaving me in full charge unless, in the
meantime, I asked him to return. It was a very tempting
offer and I was inclined to accept it, but I was very much
attached to Mr. Sinclair, to whom I had every reason to be
grateful, and so firmly convinced of the verity of the axiom
that "a rolling stone gathers no moss" that I made up my
mind to continue with my contract work, and I did.

I entered into a contract with Sinclair and Wells to
do logging approximately fifty miles farther up the river
than we had lumbered before, and established two camps
in the very heart of the wilderness near the head waters
of the Escanaba. These became the outposts between
the lumbering region of Green Bay and the Lake Superior
copper region, which was then in the early stages of development. I remained here for five months, during which time
we had no vegetables or fresh meat, subsisting entirely on
salt pork and beans except for the luxury that was afforded
the camps once or twice by the slaughter of an ox. Despite
the monotony of our fare and the severe conditions, the
health of the men was excellent and they were none the
worse for the experience.[1] In the spring when I brought
down the drive I weighed more than ever before.

We reached the mill with the logs about the middle
of May, 1852, and there I found Mr. Billings, who again

[1] In the earlier days in New Brunswick the lack of vegetables sometimes resulted
in outbreaks of scurvy or "black-leg" and in Maine codfish and potatoes boiled
together were packed in barrels and supplied to the camps to replace the salt pork.
In Wisconsin and Michigan, however, we escaped the disease, although at one time,
while logging on the Menominee, I suspected that we were threatened with it.

made me the offer of a partnership if I would take charge
of his business. Perhaps I lacked the courage, perhaps
the good sense, to take it. Doubtless I was much influenced
in my decision by the fact that prospects in other directions were brightening and I had begun to enjoy the first
measure of success. From the operations of the vessel,
"Cleopatra," in the summer time, I had made a profit, and
the logging contracts had turned out very well. Taking
advantage of the opportunity to enjoy a bit of leisure, for
the first time in seven years, I placed a captain in charge of
the vessel, as I have said, and went back East.

The rapidity with which the country was developing
was strikingly reflected in the changes that had taken
place in those seven years. Since my first arrival in Milwaukee the railroad had been constructed from Chicago
to Monroe, Michigan, whence one journeyed by steamer
to Dunkirk, New York, the terminus of the Erie Railroad
from New York City. I went on to Boston by rail and from
Boston to Calais, Maine, by boat.

On this trip I was accompanied by two men, who had
gone from Maine to work for me in the Michigan woods
and were returning to their homes also for a visit. They
wore the regulation dress of the period, short double-
breasted jackets and caps, and I was rather more splendidly
attired in a frock coat, but for some reason our appearance
doubtless suggested that we were not of the eastern environment and people with whom we came in contact jumped to
the conclusion that we were returning from California, which
was in everybody's mind because of the discovery of gold
not long before. "You men must have struck it rich out
there," observed a baggage man who found one of our
trunks somewhat heavy. "Oh!" said McShane, one of my
companions, loftily, "we can't complain." One of the

innovations of the day was the daguerreotype, which was then just coming into vogue in the East and was, as yet, unknown in the West. The picture which I had taken in Boston on the occasion of this visit I still have in my possession. For four months I wandered care-free among the scenes of my early childhood in New Brunswick and in Maine, at the end of which I returned to Wisconsin with a number of men who were to work with me in the woods at Escanaba.

In our logging operations we had penetrated so far into the wilderness that in 1851 and 1852 our supply road came within thirty miles of Marquette and was connected with the settlement by trail. For the first time, in 1851, the mail, which had hitherto been carried on toboggans or packed on the backs of carriers, was brought to my camps by teams from Green Bay and taken thence to Ashland, Ontonagon and the vicinity on toboggans drawn by dogs. When the forest was locked in the grip of winter and the trails made impassable except on show shoes, the only outlet southward from the Lake Superior region was through my camps and over the supply road to Escanaba.

Copper mining was just beginning and there were small settlements at Eagle River and Eagle Harbor to which there was much traffic. In accordance with the rule of hospitality observed in these faraway corners the travelers were welcomed to the mess table and given shelter at the camps without cost, and speeded on their way when they resumed their journey. On one occasion there were thirty-two dogs and forty-one men remaining over night on their way down the supply road to Escanaba or over the frozen trail for the north.

From this point of vantage I saw much of the development of the northern peninsula of Michigan, the gradual withdrawal of the curtain of the wilderness to reveal deposits of copper and iron which have added the cast of romance to the history of this remarkable region. How little one may scrutinize the future is reflected in the negotiations which resulted in the inclusion of this territory in the State of Michigan. In adjusting differences which had arisen between this state and Ohio over their dividing line, Michigan was induced to yield its claim over the southeastern portion of its territory, and by way of compensation was given the upper peninsula. A storm of protest was aroused over the transaction, and statesmen declared that the region was worthless. In the wake of the trapper and Indian trader came the lumbermen. Floating or mass copper pointed the way to deposits of that metal, and the discovery of iron followed. The worthless region had scarcely been surveyed before it began to add millions to the wealth of the country. And I, for one, am of the belief that its hidden resources are far from being fully disclosed. Where there is one iron mine now there may be hundreds in time.

In 1848, two years after I arrived at Flat Rock for the first time, the only iron mine known west of Pennsylvania was the Jackson mine at Negaunee. Its meager output, an excellent quality of ore, was hauled twelve miles to Marquette, where small furnaces had been established by E. K. Collins, who was interested in transatlantic shipping, and smelted into blooms. Subsequently a plank road was built from Negaunee to Marquette, an undertaking in which I narrowly escaped taking part, and eventually the railroads were built. Other iron mines were discovered at Ishpeming, Champion and elsewhere, and more on the headwaters of the Menominee River, and the output of the region has kept pace with the tremendous development in the iron and steel industry.

In the winter of 1851–52, while lumbering on the upper Escanaba, we used sand to retard the progress of the sleighs down a small hill on one of the branch roads. In the sand was slate ore. To the discovery I gave little thought at the time; but it remained in my mind, and during the war I told Mr. Smith, the discoverer of many iron deposits in the upper peninsula, about it and asked him to make an examination of the prospect. This he did not do until 1868, when he found on our supply road a mile from where I had come upon the slate a good quality of ore near the surface. On this site is the Princeton mine, formerly called the Smith mine. On the lands where I discovered the first indications, a good body of ore was discovered two hundred and sixty feet from the surface with the diamond drill. Here the Stephenson and other mines have since been established.

The isolated outpost where we camped in the early fifties has had, therefore, a rather singular history. Of this unusual destiny, however, we had no inkling at the time. We did our work as we found it, living according to the simple routine of the logging camps and driving only at the one purpose, the production of lumber, in which respect it differed little from many other camps which had played a less important part in the development of the upper peninsula.

In this environment we were without many of the advantages — and disadvantages — of a more accessible and settled community. There was no place except for those who were engaged in the actual business at hand. Doctors were few, lawyers were fewer, and preachers were rare in the entire region, and, strange as it may seem from the present point of view, we did very well without them.

One of the few physicians on the upper peninsula was a Dr. Clark, a man about thirty-five years of age and a graduate of Harvard University, who was stationed at Eagle River. In lieu of fees he was paid seven dollars a month by each man in the community, which made in the aggregate a considerable income according to the standards of the time. Although there was no great need of his services, his presence seemed to create a demand for medical attention, and to give the impression that he was serving a definite purpose he made pills of bread, which he rolled into pellets of ordinary size and flavored with a trace of aloes to produce a bitter taste.

As an illustration of the efficacy of this sham remedy he cited the case of an Irishman who came to his office one day complaining of illness. Dr. Clark went through the usual diagnosis, felt his pulse and looked at his tongue, but could discover no symptoms of any kind.

"Now, Mike," he said gravely after this operation, "I think I can bring you around all right if you will follow my instructions carefully. Take one of these now," he added, producing the bread pellets, "and another at four o'clock this afternoon. If you are no better in a day or two, come in again."

The psychological effects of this treatment were sufficient to bring about the desired result. The next day the doctor in making his rounds saw the Irishman at work and asked him how he felt. "Oh, I'm all right now, Doctor!" said the patient. "The pills cured me." In justification of this practice Doctor Clark said that the men demanded something for the money they paid him, and it was much easier to give it to them than to attempt to convince them that they were not ailing. I have since observed that this is generally true, and I am disposed to regard as still undecided the question whether disease does not follow in the wake of doctors rather than doctors in the wake of disease.

Dr. Clark came to the camp over the trail on a toboggan drawn by a half-breed with the assistance of three dogs,—one of the many who came and went between the frozen North and the settled country below. From some of them I purchased snowshoes, which they abandoned at the camp when they took the supply road for the mouth of the river.

The winter of 1851 and 1852 was unusually severe. At Marquette there was seven feet of snow, at Escanaba five and one-half feet, and over the Lake Superior settlements the shadow of famine hovered ominously close before the opening of navigation. At Marquette especially there was a scarcity of provisions and the people found it difficult to maintain themselves, the last boat of the previous season having failed to make its appointed trip. Because of the lack of supplies thirty-five horses were sent to our camp. Three were abandoned on the way when the feed began to give out; the remaining thirty-two we purchased for eight dollars each, with the exception of three or four for which we paid thirty-two dollars. Nor were the animals the only occupants of Marquette to suffer. The Rev. William A. Benson, the first Methodist minister, whose larder was exhausted, made his way to the camp also and I gave him a supply of pork to tide him over the winter until the opening of navigation enabled boats to come to the rescue of the isolated village.

Except for such untoward accidents as this, the unusual severity of the winter brought no great hardship. Travel continued through the camps unchecked and oftentimes our quarters were crowded with men who adapted themselves cheerfully to the harsh conditions of their environment. One night in midwinter two men, one a half-breed, the other a Frenchman, instead of remaining under shelter went to the outskirts of the camp and with three pairs of heavy blankets made a bed on the snow, giving as a reason for this odd choice that the camp was too warm and that as they were accustomed to sleeping out-of-doors it would be unwise for them to break the rule by yielding to the blandishment of shelter and a fire for a single night. The men who carried the mails likewise preferred to sleep out in the open in the frosty air.

The greatest discomfort of winter travel was due to the fact that it was impossible to do any cooking on the way. Fires could not be built on the snow, and it was difficult to find a log or bit of brush jutting through the thick covering to serve as foundation on which a few embers could be laid sufficiently long to boil even the water necessary for tea. Conditions, therefore, forced us to subsist on cold fare. For all of these apparent hardships the voyagers suffered little with rheumatism or any other of the ailments supposed to result from exposure of this kind.

In April, 1852, I went with one of my men from my camps to Marquette to make a survey for a road from Negaunee to the Escanaba River which Mr. Sinclair contemplated building. The trail was well beaten down with frequent travel, but in the untracked forest through which my route lay the snow was still five feet deep and we were equipped with snowshoes. On April 9 I left Negaunee with a Mr. Duncan, of Chicago, one of the first men to become interested in copper mining at Isle Royal, to trace the road southward. Duncan was a man of great energy and was connected with many business ventures. At the time he had under consideration a plan to construct a plank road to provide an outlet for the ore from the Jackson mine, which at this time was hauled to Marquette where small furnaces had been established. At the age of twenty-one he had sailed a ship out of Boston and had later founded the town of Massillon, Ohio. His son-in-law, Herman B. Ely, was one of the members of the firm of Ely and Daishla, wholesale grocers, of Buffalo and Chicago, then generally known throughout the West.

Mr. Duncan came with me as far as Goose Lake, about five miles southeast of Negaunee in the heart of the wilderness, where we parted after drinking tea together. I continued on my way to the Escanaba, tracing a road as I went, and emerged near my first camp, in the vicinity of which several iron mines have been developed, among them the Stephenson and Princeton mines, leased and operated by the Cleveland-Cliffs Company. When we arrived at the river the snow had melted to a depth of three and one-half feet.

During the following summer I had under consideration two proposals which appealed to me: one made by Mr. Duncan to enter into partnership with him in the construction of the plank road from Negaunee to Marquette, the other to take charge, as a partner, of the property of Messrs. Wright and Holbrook at Sturgeon River, now Nahma, on Big Bay de Noc. I went through to Sturgeon River on July 4, 1853, to meet Mr. Wright, who intended to come from Chicago by way of Washington Harbor. He was taken ill in Chicago, however, and compelled to abandon the trip. After waiting for him for two or three days I returned to Escanaba and found there awaiting me Mr. Duncan, who had come up on one of the vessels of the N. Ludington Company which had succeeded the Sinclair and Wells Company.

Carrying packs and accompanied by one of my men, we followed the supply road to a point where the Princeton mine was developed later, and thence over the trail to Marquette, arriving at our destination the third day. The journey was far more difficult than the one I had made some time before when the snow was on the ground. Mr. Duncan had injured his leg three months before while boarding a vessel at the "Soo," and walked with difficulty, and carried a supply of towels which he wet and bound about his shin to alleviate the pain. Besides, he was sixty-eight years of age. Our progress, therefore, was slow, and to make matters worse the mosquitos swarmed about us in clouds.

On the third day, when we were a little east of Swansea, Mr. Duncan became faint and I decided to make tea to refresh and revive him. In this plight, however, we were without water. The only available supply was that which lay in the little bogs, which were numerous in this part of the country, but it was thick and stagnant and yellow. I strained two quarts of it through the corner of my blanket, the residuum being a pint of tadpoles of various size and with it, foul-smelling and unpalatable as it was, brewed the tea. It had the desired effect. Mr. Duncan after a brief rest revived, and we continued our journey none the worse for our unsavory brew.

We made a survey of the route for the plank road and came to an agreement that I was to have a half interest in the enterprise and to take full charge of the work at a large salary. We signed a contract to this effect on July 13, 1853, with the proviso, however, that it was to become effective only in the event that I could make an arrangement with my partner, David Langley, for the sale of my interest in our logging equipment. I suspected that Mr. Sinclair, who wished me to remain with the company in one capacity or another, would find a way to prevent my leaving if he could. This suspicion was well founded. Upon my return to Escanaba I found that he had purchased Langley's interest in the logging outfit and was unwilling to make an arrangement by which I could be released. I wrote to Mr. Duncan at Cleveland, explaining the situation and expressing regret at the untoward outcome of our planning.

CHAPTER IX

Prosperity of the early fifties — High cost of living — Beginning of work on the canal at the "Soo" — "King" Strang and the Mormon colony on Beaver Island — Production of timber for breakwater at Chicago — Establishment of camps on the Menominee River — Cholera epidemic in the Middle West — Narrow escape from the disease — Extensive logging operations at Masonville.

DURING the period from 1853 to 1857, when the country was on the crest of a wave of prosperity, I followed in the wake of expanding opportunity. Lumber was in demand everywhere. Prices were high, and the industry, which was in its infancy in the Middle West but a few years before, began to thrive and develop by leaps and bounds. So great was the need for men who knew the practical side of lumbering that during this time, and for several years before, I received numerous tempting proposals to take charge of properties at Muskegon, White Lake, Manistee, Marquette, even Oconto and elsewhere, all of which I declined. In most instances, however, I procured men who were able to measure up to the requirements of these places, many of whom were successful and became prominently identified with the communities which grew up around them.

Of late it has become the custom to accentuate even the measure of prosperity we enjoyed and, by way of comparison, to regard the high cost of living as a very recent development. Such was not altogether the case. Provisions were higher in the fifties than at any time since. My old account books show that the average price of pork was from twenty-five to thirty-five dollars a barrel, spring wheat flour from six to nine dollars a barrel, calico from twelve to fifteen cents a yard. The price of sugar was twice as much as it is at present and other staple commodities were proportionately higher. Most of the added cost of living arises from the addition to the list of household and personal supplies of articles which we regarded as luxuries and had no place in our manner of living but which, according to the extravagant view of the present time, are looked upon as necessities.

We did enjoy a decided advantage, however, in the low price of fish, which were very plentiful. In the forties and later there were several thousand fishermen, who used commonly Mackinaw boats, around Green Bay settlements, along the straits of Mackinac and in the vicinity of the islands in this region. The Narrows at the entrance of Bay de Noquette was a favorite fishing ground for trout. It was said that one Edward Light caught three hundred of them in a single day, fishing with a hook through a hole in the ice. Whitefish I have purchased for our lumbering establishments for two cents per pound by the ton, delivered at the company store. The supply of them in the northern waters of the great lakes appeared to be inexhaustible, but with the advent of pound nets they began to dwindle, until there is now but one where there were thousands before. Sometimes they were so numerous in the rapids on the Escanaba River that the mills were shut down to enable the men to make a catch. Trout also were abundant in the small lakes and streams, but they have decreased in numbers as the fishermen have penetrated the out-of-the-way places.

Mr. Sinclair having blocked my scheme of building the plank road from Negaunee to Marquette by the purchase of David Langley's interest in my logging outfit, which he doubtless conceived to be to my own advantage, I resumed again the business of looking up and entering pine lands, for which purpose he desired mainly to retain my services. Men who had the experience and equipment to do this were rare in the upper peninsula, and at this time the scramble for accessible timber was much more keen than it had been a few years before. The tracts most advantageously situated along the lower reaches of the rivers and streams emptying into Green Bay had been generally taken up and it was necessary to penetrate farther into the depths of the forests.

Searching out pine timber,— the hard woods and lesser growths were of little value,— and running a line to ascertain the location was no small task. Most of the mill owners were hard put to it to find men to do this kind of work and to enter the land at the land office. The difficulty was increased by the unscrupulousness of the recorders employed by the federal government. It was the rule rather than the exception that the explorer who had undergone privation and hardship to find the timber, when he came to enter it at the land office was met with the statement of the recorder that it had already been entered. This, of course, was not true. The recorder had a list of willing "dummies" always at hand who were put down as the purchasers of the property, which was afterward sold at a neat profit to himself and his co-conspirators who supplied the money. The foundations of not a few American fortunes were laid in this reprehensible fashion.

About this time the State of Michigan had granted large tracts to the "Soo" Land Company for canal purposes, and it was the aim of Mr. Sinclair to look these over before the transfer of title was actually made. I hurried

to the Menominee River to look over some lands and enter
them at the Menasha land office,— the first to be entered
in that region,— and then to the "Soo" to look over those
involved in the canal grant.

In the meantime, Messrs. Wright and Holbrook, of
Nahma, were still desirous of having me take an interest
with them, and after my return from Wisconsin it was my
purpose to go to Nahma to discuss terms with them. The
wind, however, was contrary and after waiting for some
time in vain for favorable weather, I boarded my own vessel,
the "Cleopatra," and went to Milwaukee. I wrote to Mr.
Wright, declining his proposition, and recommended for
the place Jefferson S. Bagley, a nephew of Mr. Sinclair
and a very capable man, who took charge of the business.
He arrived at Nahma with a number of men and women
and winter supplies on the schooner "Juliet Patten,"
on December 11, 1853. Because of the lateness of the
season, and the lack of tugs to break the ice in the harbor, the journey was hazardous but was completed without
mishap.

In October I left for the "Soo" to enter the lands for
the N. Ludington Company. I went by rail to Detroit
and there met Robert Graveraet, who played a conspicuous
part in the development of the upper peninsula as the
agent for eastern copper interests, and who first pitched
his tent in the wilderness on the site of the present city of
Marquette. He informed me that a boat was to leave for
the "Soo" the following morning on which I secured a
reservation in the after cabin on the main deck. On the
same vessel, the "Detroit," of the Ward line, the first party
of workmen who were to dig the canal had, with their
families, taken passage. They were all Irish. At this
time the people of no other nation seemed to have ac-

quired proficiency in excavation work of this character, and the emigrants from the Emerald Isle, who were especially adept in the use of the shovel, scattered over the United States, and other countries to a smaller extent, wherever construction work was being carried on. They built the railroads in France and in this country, dug canals in Pennsylvania and were exclusively engaged for the work about to be undertaken at the "Soo."

We ran into a gale on Lake Huron and were somewhat apprehensive, because the boat was old and said to be overloaded, but weathered the storm safely and arrived at our destination on November 3, when the first shovelful of soil was taken out of the canal, which was opened in September, 1855. One of my fellow passengers on this trip was Mr. Duncan whom I had not seen since I made the futile contract with him for the construction of the plank road.

After entering lands at the "Soo" I returned to Milwaukee, setting sail on the steamer "Garden City." This ill-fated vessel, running in opposition to the Ward Line between Chicago and the "Soo," was lost the following year between Mackinac and Detour, on what has since been called the Garden City Reef, in commemoration of the disaster. I remember my voyage on the boat with peculiar distinctness because of an incident which occurred at Beaver Island, where we stopped to take on wood.

This community had been established at an early day by the Mormons, at the head of whom was John Strang, a rather extraordinary figure in this period of Michigan history, known as "King" Strang to his faithful subjects. The colony had removed some years before from Rochester, near Kenosha, Wisconsin, through which I had passed in 1846, to Beaver Island, where they were held in great awe by the people of the surrounding country and by mariners on the lakes, who believed that they not only followed a strange creed, but were guilty of outrageous if not criminal practices. This idea, needless to say, was without basis and was due to misleading and malicious rumors to which the yarn-spinning sailors, I have no doubt, added as they congregated about the stoves in their winter haunts when navigation was closed. The Mormons were really a hard-working and patient people who did not molest their neighbors; but the fishermen and wood-choppers who competed with them, some of whom were fugitives from the eastern states, were very bitter and spread reports that they had killed a number of persons and that one or two vessels said to have been wrecked in the vicinity of Beaver Island had really been seized by them, the crews murdered and the cargoes taken as plunder.

We arrived at Beaver Island in the evening with only two or three passengers aboard. While we were negotiating for the purchase of wood, "King" Strang came aboard apparently to make a friendly visit. Captain Squires, who had heard the evil reports about the Mormons, had misgivings about their leader and was prepared to keep on the alert until he was out of sight. Strang, however, showed no disposition to leave in a hurry — very naturally, as he was waiting until the wood had been loaded. Two of us kept watch with the captain, and to break our vigil refreshed ourselves at midnight with roasted potatoes and buttermilk in his cabin. At that time Strang was still aboard. Captain Squires then decided to try a plan I had suggested to be rid of him. He bargained with the Mormon leader for twenty more cords of wood, and, having arrived at an agreement, said that as his men were tired and it was necessary to make repairs to one of the wheels he would not load it until the following day. Strang left the boat to make preparations and the captain stealthily slipped off his lines at three o'clock in the morning and headed for Milwaukee. Captain Squires, who had been in command of the steamer "Arrow," the loss of which on the Hudson, near West Point, in 1845 was one of the great catastrophes of the period, afterward managed the Madison House in Chicago for many years.

After my arrival at Milwaukee the N. Ludington Company entered into contracts with the Illinois Central Railroad for the production of square timber for the breakwater on the lake front at Chicago. How much this improvement was needed can scarcely be conceived by those who know only the expansive stretch of parking and intricate web of railroad tracks faced by the huge buildings of Michigan Avenue of later years. Before it was built the waves driven by a northeast gale sometimes lapped the doorsteps of the houses, many of them wooden structures, which bordered this thoroughfare. The city, too, has since stealthily encroached upon the water. In 1848, at the foot of Lake Street, a point now far inland, we lost a vessel which was blown ashore on April 22, the crew saving themselves by jumping from the jib boom to the sandy beach. In other respects also, far from being the metropolis it has since become, it was not an attractive city. Planking took the place of pavement. High wooden sidewalks, necessities in view of the boggy nature of the soil, lined Randolph and other streets, and oftentimes when I drove from our lumber yard on the West Side my horse plodded through a batter of mud in sections where the din of traffic now echoes among the tall buildings.

The construction of the breakwater was an important undertaking measured according to the standards of the time. To carry the timber we built a vessel of special design, called the "Alexander Mitchell," at Port Huron, with ports so arranged that the timber could be hoisted into the hold. The brig "C. I. Hutchins" was also purchased and equipped in the same manner. At this time the "donkey" engine was unknown and horses were carried on the decks of vessels to do the hoisting, a very cumbersome arrangement, as might be imagined. In a gale, when footing was uncertain, the poor animals were thrown and lashed to the decks, a practice which led to the use by sailors of the phrase: "Six men and two horses before the mast." The donkey engine did not come into use until oil was discovered. William B. Ogden purchased thirteen of them at an auction at Corry, Pennsylvania, and sold them to contractors who used them for driving piles at Chicago and other ports on the lakes.

Some of the timber used on the breakwaters at Chicago, Sturgeon River and other harbors on the lakes we cut on Sand Point, the site of the present city of Escanaba, but the greater portion of it was taken from the forests along the Menominee River. The company, after my return from the "Soo," had made arrangements for me to take a crew of men to the latter region. We left Milwaukee on a vessel laden with supplies and arrived at the mouth of the river on November 11, 1853, at five o'clock in the morning.

I piloted the ship to its anchorage and after unloading the supplies and logging equipment went ten miles up the river and established the first camp. Later I established two more and during the winter of 1853 and 1854 directed the operations of eighty men who made timber thirteen inches square which was counter-hewed to twelve inches in Chicago. The minimum length was twenty-five feet but much of it was more than thirty and some sticks were

seventy-five feet. In addition to directing the work of
the timber crews and measuring timber I did much exploring.
For twenty-five nights during the winter, which was unusually severe, my brother and I slept in the open forest
without shelter while on our expeditions. For three days
during a cold wave the thermometer fell to thirty-five
degrees below zero and at Green Bay city it was said to have
been forty below. Three of my men were badly frozen.

After several months of hard work I took passage
on June 13, 1854, from Menominee to Chicago, on one of
the vessels, the "Alexander Mitchell," which was laden with
square timber. On the same boat was Mr. Duncan, who
had come down from Lake Superior in the latter part of
March. He was dissatisfied with the progress of the
work on the plank road at Marquette and, old as he was,
had also conceived the plan of erecting a sawmill. We
discussed both undertakings and reached an agreement,—
a very satisfactory one from my point of view,— by which
I was to take a very large interest in and to have full charge
of the business. Assuming that the plan this time would
be carried out I even went to the extent of making arrangements to send cattle, equipment and supplies, together
with a number of men, from Escanaba to Marquette as
soon as I had completed my work on the Menominee.

Some time after my arrival in Chicago, I went to see
Mr. Ely, Mr. Duncan's son-in-law, who lived on Park Row,
at that time the fashionable residence section of the city.
He informed me that Mr. Duncan was ill but would see me
some time during the afternoon. The visit was the last
I paid the indefatigable pioneer. As I sat by his bedside
he informed me that he had been obliged to abandon the
project of building the mill because the land grant to the
Northwestern Railroad, which had been changed from

the western to the eastern portion of Delta and Marquette counties, had covered the timber he intended to purchase. He had written to me, he said, to this effect but the letter had never reached its destination. So ended my second attempt to transfer my activities to the Lake Superior region. Before I left Mr. Duncan expressed the hope that he would be himself again in a few days but this did not come to pass. Although he lived for a number of years afterward at Marquette he never fully recovered from his illness and the projects he conceived were never carried out.

On the day after this visit, as I was about to leave for Milwaukee with my brother, S. M. Stephenson and two or three other men, Samuel Hamilton, the owner of the property at Cedar River, hailed me in the omnibus and persuaded me to remain over for a day. With him I went to the office of Holt and Mason, who owned the mill at Masonville, north of Gladstone, Michigan, and within the hour I had made a contract with Mr. R.D. Holt, the Chicago manager of the firm, to supply them with all the logs required by their plant. They were also in need of some one to survey timber lands and on my arrival at Milwaukee I sent my brother with several men to Masonville for this purpose while I myself went on to the "Soo" to examine the maps at the land office to ascertain which lands were vacant and could be entered.

I returned to Chicago by way of Detroit for a consultation with Mr. Holt. The day of my arrival, July 7, 1854, was one not easily to be forgotten. It was marked by the death of one hundred and thirty-nine people, among them Mr. Ely, Mr. Duncan's son-in-law, victims of the cholera. The fear of the epidemic, which assumed the proportions of a plague, was upon us all and the city was overshadowed with gloom. For five years it claimed thousands of victims in the Middle West, taking heaviest toll of the towns and cities.

Three or four days elapsed before one of our boats left for the mills, during which time I remained at the Briggs House. When I did go aboard the vessel I became ill, having all the symptoms of the dread disease, and for the first and only time in my life I began to fear that the shadow of death was upon me. None the less I was not willing just then to abandon the struggle. The chances being against me I was willing to compromise with fate if it spared me until we had passed Death's Door so that I might be taken to Escanaba where my family awaited me and I struggled as valiantly as I could against the pain which beset me. A money belt in which I carried four or five hundred dollars in gold and which caused much discomfort I turned over to the captain. Crouching beside the bed in my cabin I gathered what little power of resistance remained to me to hold off what seemed to be the approaching end.

Not long afterward the pain diminished, the crisis passed and the illness disappeared almost as suddenly and unaccountably as it came. By the time we arrived at Masonville I was myself again except for the weakness due to the ordeal through which I had passed. Without tarrying to recuperate I put my knapsack on my back and went at once with my men into the woods. In two days I had regained my strength and worked so energetically at running lines that my companions were hard put to it to keep up with me. During this period my diet consisted of pork and dry bread. For three months I continued my explorations for timber for Holt and Mason making rapid progress because of my experience and knowledge of the country.

About this time my operations were begun on a very large scale. In October I entered into a contract to supply logs to the mills on Day's and Rapid rivers and purchased all of the sleighs, teams, and camp equipment of Holt and Mason including thirty-three oxen and twenty horses and four or five dozen buffalo robes worth from forty to forty-five dollars a dozen, which were used in lieu of blankets.

CHAPTER X

Responsibilities of camp management — Experiences in medicine and surgery — Adjusting disputes — Lack of machinists — I leave Mr. Sinclair — Negotiations for purchase of interest in Masonville property — Changes in Sinclair and Wells company — Death of Mr. Sinclair — Panic of 1857 — Purchase of interest in N. Ludingtom Company at Marinette.

THE responsibilities I bore at this time covered a much wider range than the mere direction of logging activities. In the camps and at the settlements around the mills, far removed from the communities where there was an organized system of local government, the superintendent or "boss" was as absolute as the captain of a vessel on the high seas. He settled all disputes, maintained order, took care of the sick and regulated affairs generally. Nor was there any constituted authority upon which he could depend for the enforcement of his decrees. For this he had to rely upon his own resources.

The most important task was probably the care of the sick and injured. In Maine the medicine chest had been one of the indispensable requisites of the camp equipment, and Mr. Sinclair always had one at hand when he began operations in Michigan. Following his example I had become somewhat adept in treating illnesses and devoted much time to reading such literature on the subject of medical practice as was available. Sickness, fortunately, was rare but the men not infrequently injured themselves while working on frozen timber, many gashes being inflicted by glancing axes, and it was necessary under these primitive conditions to act as surgeon by sewing up the wounds. These minor operations were performed successfully and every patient recovered as promptly and with as few complications as might be expected under modern hospital conditions.

From 1854 to 1858, when I was supplying all the logs for Holt and Mason at Little Bay de Noc, I employed one hundred and twenty men in the winter, besides the mill crews and women and children, and at White Fish, four miles from Masonville, more than a hundred men, besides women and children,— in all about one thousand persons. During these four years I lost only two men by sickness. One of them, who was inexperienced in the ways of camp life, worked only for a day when he was taken down with erysipelas, froze his toes while cutting wood for an hour and lost five or six of them. From this plight I succeeded in rescuing him and he was apparently on the road to complete recovery, except for the missing toes, when in violation of the instructions given him he ate a quantity of pork and greasy food which caused a protracted illness resulting in death. The only other fatal case was that of a young man who contracted an intestinal disease which did not yield to our rudimentary treatment.

My experiences in medicine and surgery did not end here. At Marinette, where there were doctors, there was more or less for me to do in the way of assisting at, if not actually performing, surgical operations, some of them amputations of a serious character. Dr. Hall, one of the pioneer lumbermen of the Menominee, who came from Ithaca, New York, in the early forties, although not actively engaged in the practice of medicine, responded to the call of necessity and treated the sick and injured of the community as occasion required. He guided his course

by the philosophy that the less the medicine the better for
the patient and his surgical work he confined to the unavoidable minimum. Oftentimes he said to me: "I don't
want to meet these people hereafter and have them tell
me that I made cripples of them." Sometimes when men
were severely injured we could not avoid amputation altogether, but we did as little as possible using, for lack of
better instruments, carpenters' tools. The general conclusion I have reached as a result of these experiences
is that much of the activity of doctors is superfluous and
many of the operations they perform unnecessary. But
that subject I leave for others to discuss.

Unaided I performed what was probably the first
amputation in Marinette about 1860. One of the men employed in the mill at Menekaunee mangled his hand in the
machinery and it was necessary to cut off the arm about
four inches above the wrist. Dr. Hall was unable to perform the operation and it was necessary for me to act as
surgeon. There was no anæsthetic. The unfortunate
victim of the accident was conscious all of the time. A tool
chest afforded most of our instruments and the sterilizing
apparatus of the modern operating room was unknown.
None the less the patient came through the ordeal without
mishap and lived for twenty years afterwards. There
were a number of accidents of this kind necessitating amputation which Dr. Hall or I performed. We cut as little
as possible and succeeded as well as a surgeon under modern
conditions could have done.

It is certain, at least, that for the most part we did
very well without doctors. In 1877, when the N. Ludington Company was constructing what was known as the
Dow dam, near Amberg, Wisconsin, we employed sixty
men. I invited Dr. Jones, of Marinette, to inspect the

camp with me and, while we were eating our breakfast in
three inches of snow without shelter of any kind, we discussed conditions and the health of the men. "There
are sixty of them here," I said, "who have been at work
for six weeks. During that time not one of them has been
sick. Two jammed their feet without any serious permanent effects, but that was all. If they had been at the
mill at the village where there were doctors and drug stores
and newspapers advertising patent medicines for all kinds
of ailments I have no doubt that at least three or four every
day would have thought that they required drugs." Dr.
Jones, possibly with some reluctance, admitted the truth
of the assertion.

In other respects also we succeeded in getting on very
comfortably without many of the institutions that are
now considered essential to the life of a community. At
Escanaba and Masonville for twelve years, until 1858, we
had neither doctors, lawyers, nor ministers. Neither did
we feel that we were suffering very much for lack of them
except, possibly, the ministers. I believed then, as I do
now, that it would have been an advantage, perhaps a
consolation, to the people to have some one preach the
gospel to them and to administer to their spiritual wants.
Whatever their creed might have been their influence
would have been for good.

Because of the lack of lawyers and the difficulty of
resorting to ordinary legal processes for the settlement of
private difficulties we were free from the burdens which
litigation oftentimes imposes upon a community. There
were no divorces whatever. What domestic disturbance
arose it fell to the lot of the superintendent to settle. This
summary method was much more effective than the modern
remedy offered by the courts. I have no doubt that

many families would have been dispersed and homes broken up — there was ample occasion for disagreement — if the legal machinery of to-day had been available.

Fortunately it was not. The "boss" usually brought the refractory principals involved in the controversy together, scored them roundly for their misbehavior and threatened to turn them loose upon an unfriendly wilderness if they repeated the offense. Almost inevitably this treatment resulted in a promise to do better and the promise once made was carried out. I have in mind one case which illustrates the effectiveness of this summary treatment,— that of an Irishman and his wife, persons of almost gigantic stature, who became involved in a quarrel. To end the fracas and save herself, the woman, with both eyes blackened, took refuge in my house. The husband, becoming penitent over night, came the next day to see her, but I told him as gravely as I could that the camp had been so aroused by his brutal treatment of his wife that it was bent upon giving him a coat of tar and feathers and that it would be well for him to hide himself in the woods for two or three days until the feeling subsided. He was thoroughly frightened and did as I suggested. In the meantime I took the wife in hand and by a process of admonition brought her to the stage of penitence and alarm over the non-appearance of her husband. In time she returned to her home where her husband joined her and for two years afterward they lived together in perfect serenity, models of domestic virtue.

There was another phase of lumbering at this time which can be understood only by those who have knowledge of the difficulties of keeping a mill in operation. We were far removed from the sources of supply and our equipment was meager compared to the establishments of the

present. If a part needed replacing or repairs were to be
made we had to rely upon our own resources. For this
reason the blacksmith shop and the carpenter shop were
an integral part of the establishment and a knowledge of
smithing was almost essential to the superintendent who
was at times called upon to forge chains, make axes and
other tools, and shape broken parts. At Escanaba the
company was fortunate to have as a blacksmith William
Rogers, a man of many attainments outside his profession,
who built the Flat Rock dam. I have known him to forge
a knife in the morning, grind it and make a handle for it
and shave the men with it in the afternoon.

For the more important repairs it was necessary to
have machinists, who were in great demand. Two of the
best of them on the upper lakes were Mason and Barber,
who had come to Grand Haven from England by way of
Canada. Both were exceedingly skillful in those days when
it was necessary to work with a hammer and cold chisel,
such machine tools as lathes not having come into use.
Mr. Barber bought out the interest of Mr. Mason,— who
was afterwards associated with Mr. Holt in the firm of
Holt and Mason,— at Grand Haven and was able to retire within a short time with a considerable fortune which
he enlarged in Chicago, where he was rated as one of the
wealthy men of the city. He returned to Europe in 1858,
with his wife and one child, to visit his home in England.
On their return the steamer "Pacific," on which they had
taken passage, was lost with all on board. His estate was
dissipated not long afterward.

When I undertook logging operations for Holt and
Mason I necessarily severed my connection with Mr.
Sinclair. This I did with much regret, for I was mindful
of all that he had done for me and how much my own prog-

ress had depended upon the lessons he had taught me. He was also sorry to have me go but there was no other prospect unless I continued to work for him on a salary basis, which I was not content to do. He and the members of his family, however, remained my steadfast friends. The agreement he had made that I should be given a farm and equipment was never carried out. Mrs. Sinclair volunteered to make good the promise after Mr. Sinclair's death, but I declined her offer.

Mr. Mason was an excellent millwright and his partner, Mr. Holt, who had charge of the lumber yard in Chicago, was a very capable business man and they made a good combination but neither of them had had any experience in logging or in looking up timber lands. This was left to me. Having acquired considerable capital I contemplated purchasing Mr. Mason's interest in the firm and in July, 1857, made an agreement with him by which I was to pay one-third down and the remainder in one and two years. He was to give me a deed of the property and accept a mortgage for the unpaid balance. Arrangements having been concluded on this basis I took an inventory of the goods in the store and warehouse, made contracts with jobbers and started men to work in the woods. Likewise, assuming that the bargain had been struck, Mason proceeded to dismantle his home and brought his furniture down to the dock to take the last boat of the season from Masonville for Chicago.

As he was about to leave he submitted to me, much to my amazement, what was known at the time as the "Chicago cut-throat contract" by the terms of which if a payment became overdue one became a tenant at will and forfeited all that had been paid up to that time. Reminding Mr. Mason of his agreement to give me a deed and accept a mortgage for the balance I refused to sign the contract. He admitted that such was the understanding but gave as an excuse that some years before when he had sold his property at Grand Haven he had been obliged during a panic when he was badly in need of money to wait for the payments for two years and did not wish to place himself in a similar position again. "I refuse to sign that contract," said I decisively. Equally unyielding he carted his furniture back to his dismantled house and the boat departed for Chicago without him. Again did my plans to enter into large fields of activity as a mill owner come to nothing.

In the meantime changes had taken place in the ownership and management of the business of Sinclair and Wells at Escanaba. In the winter of 1850 Harrison and Nelson Ludington, under the firm name of N. Ludington and Company, who had maintained a lumber yard at Milwaukee in which Mr. Sinclair and Mr. Wells were interested, purchased the controlling half-interest in the Sinclair and Wells Company which, in 1851, also became known as the N. Ludington Company. In the following year they opened a lumber yard at Chicago, which I helped to establish, on Twelfth Street and the South Branch, subsequently removing to a tract of land on Twenty-second Street.

In June, 1855, Mr. Sinclair under stress of an illness which affected his mind, withdrew from the business entirely and retired to Janesville. This marked the end of his rather remarkable career. In a fit of melancholia he committed suicide on his farm near Janesville in October, 1855.

In 1856 the N. Ludington Company, in addition to their property at Escanaba, erected on Mission Point, on the Menominee River, another mill, which was operated for only two months when the panic of 1857 turned the business world into a shambles and it was closed down.

Neither of the Ludingtons nor Daniel Wells, who remained in partnership with them, had the slightest knowledge of the practical side of lumbering and about the time I was negotiating with Holt and Mason they approached me with a proposition to take charge of their mills and an interest in the business. It was my judgment at the time that the Holt and Mason enterprise offered greater opportunities and I declined their offer but aided them to the extent of securing David Langley as superintendent of the mills at Escanaba. The discussion of these affairs required my presence in Chicago where, for the first time, I was able to indulge myself without stint in the delights of the drama. For thirty-six successive nights, excepting Sundays, I went to the theater and gave myself up unreservedly to the enjoyment of the tragedies of the period, which were much more satisfactory, to my mind, than the frothy comedies and melodramas of the present day.

The crash of 1857 brought the prosperity of the preceding few years to an abrupt end. Failure followed failure, business became stagnant and a period of "hard times," which was to endure for several years, until the shadow of the Civil War began to pass, followed. Many people suffered and I myself had to endure a period of enforced idleness. Reverses bore heavily upon those who possessed what might be regarded as fixed capital. Rather than feed them I slaughtered twenty oxen, receiving little or nothing for the beef, and sold a number of horses, of which I had many, to my brothers who were logging by contract. Others I let to various persons for their maintenance.

Despite our disagreement Mr. Mason and I remained good friends and went to Green Bay together from the

North on the ice with our teams in February, 1858, and thence to Fond du Lac where we boarded the train for Chicago. About March 1, I returned with Harrison Ludington, afterward Governor of Wisconsin, who contemplated starting the mill at Marinette. We remained here for a day or two for the purpose of making an arrangement to buy out the interests of Messrs. Kimball and Brown, who were associated with the Ludingtons in the ownership of the property and who also knew little about the lumber business.

Our negotiations failed at this time and we went on to Escanaba and Masonville covering eighty-two miles in a single day. About a week later we returned to Marinette, purchased from Mr. Brown his interest and secured his promise to use what influence he had to induce Mr. Kimball to relinquish his holdings also. In the meantime I returned to Masonville. On May 1, after assisting my brothers in driving their logs out of Day's and Rapid rivers, I went to Marinette with my sailboat, took the steamer to Green Bay and went by way of Fond du Lac to Chicago to complete the negotiations.

This we did successfully and I became the ower of a quarter interest in the mill, personal property and lands of the N. Ludington Company. With Mr. Ludington I returned to Marinette and took charge of the property on May 15, 1858. After more than a half-century, fifty-eight years, I am still where that venture brought me.

CHAPTER XI

Marinette in the early fifties — Queen Marinette — Menominee River becomes greatest timber producing center in the world — Difficulties due to panic of 1857 — Disappearance of forests and growth of farms — Vicissitudes of travel on Green Bay — Diversions of early lumbering villages.

THE signs of human habitation along the Menominee River when I first came to it in 1853 were few. The primeval forest, except for the small spaces cleared by the Indians and the early traders and lumbermen, came down to the water's edge; and the river, which has since been confined to narrower limits and a lower level by the dredging of channels and the improvement of the harbor, poured itself in flat volume out into the bay. The passage of larger vessels was blocked by a bar at the mouth of the stream and they were loaded or unloaded by means of smaller boats or scows while they lay at anchor some distance off shore.

On the edge of the bay on the Michigan side were probably a dozen huts occupied by white fishermen. On the site of the present city of Marinette were only three houses, one belonging to Dr. Hall, another to Queen Marinette of the Menominee tribe of Indians, and the third to her son, John B. Jacobs, one of the early traders. About a mile from the mouth of the river on the Michigan side was a large sawmill, erected by Dr. Hall in the forties and afterwards enlarged and operated by water power, and a boarding-house where the employees lived. On the opposite side was the mill erected by Farnsworth and Brush, all traces of which have since been obliterated.

Of the earlier history of the settlement few vestiges remained. Menekaunee, or Pleasant Town, where the Indian band of Te-pak-e-ne-nee, the Night Man, had established a village many years before, according to tradition, had been reclaimed by the wilderness. Arrow heads and stone implements turned up with the soil on the site of the mill and boarding-house of the N. Ludington Company, which still bears the name of Mission Point, gave evidence of the fact that the spot had been the habitat of the red men who gathered about the mission and post maintained there by the government.

There were still many Indians in the vicinity, some of whom lived in huts near the river and in small camps farther up the stream. These were removed to the reservation in Shawano in 1856. For many years afterward, however, they came to the Menominee, some of them from great distances, for fishing and hunting. One band from the Straits of Mackinac camped on the island opposite the city of Marinette some time afterward and left their squaws there while they went up the river to hunt deer, which were very plentiful, and the trail from the north was kept worn by the march of many moccasined feet.

The Menominee fishing grounds were evidently guarded with some jealousy by certain bands of Indians who resented the invasion of others of their race. There was a tradition extant in my time that one chief who was foolhardy enough to encroach upon this territory was captured and minnows were forced down his throat until he died. "If he wants fish," his captors said, "we will give him more than enough."

Queen Marinette, the descendant of a daughter of Wabashish and a French trapper named Bartholomew

Chevalière, was a capable woman, large of figure and somewhat advanced in age when I first came to the Menominee, who managed her business affairs with exceptionally good judgment although she retained many of the traits of her Indian origin. For a number of years she lived with John B. Jacobs, an English trapper and trader, who came from Canada. Later her affection for him seems to have cooled, for he relinquished whatever claim he had upon her to George Farnsworth for a pipe of high wine, and shortly afterward returned to Canada.

By the first alliance she had a son, John B. Jacobs, a very shrewd and capable man of aristocratic bearing, who devoted his time to trading and gambling. By the second there were several children. From one of them, Jane Farnsworth, I purchased a portion of Marinette's property, fronting on the river and including a portion of the heart of the city of Marinette, for fifteen twenty-dollar gold pieces. From John Jacobs, the son, I also purchased some property, now lying well within the city limits. George Farnsworth another of Marinette's children, also a man of considerable capacity, became quartermaster of the Thirty-second Regiment of Wisconsin infantry, largely upon my recommendation, during the Civil War and proved to be a very efficient officer.

Up to 1850 the timber resources along the Menominee had scarcely been touched and the extent of them was not even realized, but at that time they began to attract the attention of lumbermen and in the following decade and for some years afterward the river grew in importance until it became the greatest lumber-producing district in the world. From the few thousands of feet produced by the earlier water-mills the annual production steadily increased until it reached six and seven hundred million feet. The harvest of logs brought down with the drive in the spring extended for ten miles in solid mass along the river, and twenty-three steam mills pouring out lumber in an unending stream presented a pageant not unlike that which I as a boy had contemplated along the Penobscot from Oldtown to Bangor.

In 1855 a number of Pennsylvania and New York capitalists, associated together under the name of the New York Company, erected at the mouth of the river a large mill which encountered difficulties during the period following the panic of 1857. The next mill to be constructed was that of the N. Ludington Company on Mission Point, the site for which had been purchased by Mr. Sinclair a number of years before. It began operations in 1856, but continued for only two months when it shut down because of the financial depression. When it resumed operations on May 15, 1858, it was under my charge. From this time development went on apace and eventually my brothers, Samuel and Robert, came to the Menominee at my suggestion and occupied important positions at the head of some of these many lumbering establishments.

Casting back over the past sixty years the picture of the growth of the lumbering industry on the Menominee and the gradual recession is not without its dark shadows. The woods I traversed in the search for pine timber have practically disappeared. From many acres from which the pine was stripped in these early days I have since cut the growth of hardwood. The stream of logs driven down the river is constantly dwindling and will soon cease altogether; and the pall of silence is drawing down about the mills, which have closed one by one. The epoch of which I saw the beginning and the expansion is now coming to a somewhat melancholy close. The days of lumbering are nearly ended.

Fortunately another epoch is beginning. Farms are multiplying and green meadows and fertile fields are reaching like the fingers of a hand into the blackened waste of stumps and underbrush left to mark the passing of the chopper, and the friendly soil cleared of one harvest is yielding bountifully another. The past with its tumultuous days of development, its toil and accomplishment, has gone, and the accounting made; but the future looms big with possibilities and another half-century may see another tide of increase at its flood again.

At the time I began my career as a mill owner at Marinette, conditions were anything but favorable. The panic had brought business to a standstill. Very few men had much capital, and when the stress came many of those engaged in lumbering went to the wall. The depression that prevailed was well illustrated by a story told me by Dr. Hall at the time. When he was in Chicago in the forties during a period of "hard times," one of the men whom he had employed at the mill applied for his pay. Without regard to conditions he insisted that the doctor owed him the money and he demanded it forthwith.

"I am making provision to pay," protested Dr. Hall.

"I don't want provisions," said the Irishman. "I get all the provisions I want from you at the mill. I'll take money or nothing."

The predicament in which Dr. Hall found himself was common to almost everyone along the Menominee in the late fifties. The New York Company and the Ellsworth Company both failed, as Dr. Hall had failed earlier. The whole community was demoralized and the flow of commerce was stopped. As a basis of exchange some of the people accepted cattle, others tools. This situation was one that I had never been called upon to meet before. I and the people with whom I had been associated had always met our obligations promptly, and it was difficult to listen patiently to importunities and the stories of failure and misfortune addressed to me. Before the country had recovered from the depression following the panic, the war began and it was not until 1864 that conditions returned to a normal basis and the light of prosperity again dawned.

When we began the manufacture of lumber at Marinette in 1858, before the effects of the financial cataclysm had passed altogether, it was sold on the market at Chicago at from seven to eight dollars a thousand feet, scarcely sufficient to pay the cost of production. The stumpage represented a dead loss. The same grade of lumber to-day would be worth from thirty to thirty-five dollars a thousand. At the same time there was very little difference in the cost of sawing. What advantages have been gained and economies effected through mechanical improvements on the one hand were offset by the lower wages and longer hours on the other.

Our mill at Marinette had been hastily erected and was in constant need of alterations and repairs, and at this time men competent to look after machinery were few. This condition necessitated my working at night, very frequently, and on Sundays to avoid shutting down during the week — which would have added still further handicaps to those under which we were already laboring. I recall that on one Monday morning a religious old man in charge of a lath mill, who had observed with distrust the changes I had made on the preceding day, protested against my working on the Sabbath and predicted that no good would come of it. Before the week had ended, he said, we would pay the penalty by an accident or break of one kind or another. The prophecy did not come to pass and the mill ran without interruption or mishap of any sort — somewhat, I believe, to his disappointment.

I stuck indefatigably to the task before me and, whether by good luck or skill, acquired no indifferent reputation as a millwright. At least, the mill was kept running. The lack of mechanics and men to file the saws was the occasion of much inconvenience, but this disadvantage had no marked effect on our production. Despite the improvement in mill machinery and the increased facilities for making repairs, the average output remains proportionately the same. The competition, as I have said before, rests with the logging. Two camps under the same conditions and with the same number of men will frequently show a surprising disparity in the number of logs produced. This might be due to many things, the disabling of horses by inefficient teamsters, bad management by the "boss," dissatisfaction among the crew created by men of a certain class whom the sailors call forecastle lawyers,— in short, a variety of causes. Sawing, on the contrary, is largely a matter of mechanical precision.

Although I did not acquire an interest in the Escanaba plant of the N. Ludington Company, now called the I. Stephenson Company, until 1858, I had supervision over it in a general way and frequently made trips from Marinette to observe the progress of operations there. The vicissitudes of travel between the two points, which bore heavily upon those not accustomed to the rigors it entailed, are illustrated in one expedition I made with Nelson and Harrison Ludington and a boy named Merrick, afterward a member of the tobacco firm of Spalding and Merrick, of Chicago, during the latter part of January, 1854.

We started from Menominee in a double sleigh, the first to go north on the ice that winter. The snow was about twelve inches deep and the anchor ice had blown up in ridges in which there were crevices. When we were three and one-half miles north of Menominee, off what is now known as Poplar Point, the horse stepped into one of these crevices and broke his leg. The misfortune was a serious one. Harrison Ludington, contemplating it almost with stupefaction, exclaimed: "My God! The horse has broken his leg." In our plight the others were helpless and the burden of the mishap fell upon me. I killed the horse by striking it one or two blows in the forehead with an axe, threw the harness in the sleigh and started back for Menominee to bring a small Indian pony and more supplies. I suggested that in the meantime the others proceed on foot until overtaken. The walking was difficult because there was from three to six inches of water under the snow on the ice, and when I returned Harrison Ludington was waiting for me at the sleigh, while the others had gone only a few rods.

When we resumed the journey it was necessary for me to walk ahead to break a path through the untracked snow, exchanging places for brief intervals with Harrison Ludington. At noon we arrived at Cedar Point, built a fire and made tea. After a brief rest we headed for Cedar River, arriving at Norway Bay at evening. Cutting a way through the shore ice, which was very high, we found a deserted fisherman's camp, a small hut without windows. For fuel I cut away a part of the roof and floor, while my fellow travelers sat by commiserating one another. The chinks in the hut were stuffed with plains moss, which was very inflammable, but this fact I kept to myself.

When the fire was made I went to the bay and cut a hole in the ice, only to discover after much labor that it was too far inshore and that there was only sand at the bottom. My second attempt farther out was successful. After our meager meal I arranged beds for the others so that each had his feet toward the fire. My own was a plank. At midnight when I went out for fuel the air was clear and frosty, so frosty that an hour later I awoke to find my moccasins and stockings, wet from walking on the ice, frozen stiff. I thawed them out at the fire, and to run no further risks remained awake for the rest of the night.

We breakfasted at four o'clock and resumed our journey, arriving at Cedar River at eight o'clock. Here our troubles ended. From there Mr. Hamilton drove us to Ford River, where Mr. Sinclair joined us, and we went on to Escanaba without further mishap. On our return to Marinette, three days later, Alden Chandler accompanied us on his way to Green Bay, where he was to take the oath of office as the first postmaster of Escanaba. The Ludingtons went on to Chicago, glad that the ordeal, their only real experience with the wilderness, was over.

In this environment of hard work we had our diversions, especially on the Fourth of July and at Christmas time. On these occasions, now and then, there was a ball in which everybody joined and we danced as energetically as we worked. I have beside me the announcement of an "Independence Ball at John Quimby's new hall in Menominee, on the Fourth of July, '60," for which "the company of yourself and lady" was "respectfully solicited." The floor managers were John B. Jacobs (Queen Marinette's son) and H. K. Fowler, and the committee of arrangements representing the five towns along Green Bay were: "for Menominee, Jabez Hawkins, I. Stephenson, James Laughrey and Levi Odell; for Peshtigo, Anson Place and Levi

Hale; for Oconto, G. P. Farnsworth and George C. Ginty; for Cedar Forks, S. Hamilton and M. Boyd; and for Escanaba, D. Langley and H. Shields." These opportunities came so seldom that we made the most of them and danced from early in the evening throughout the night without pause until seven or eight o'clock the following morning.

Even this achievement was outdone on Christmas Day, 1858. We drove to the house of "Abe" Place on the Peshtigo road, arriving there about noon, took down the partition dividing the interior of the house, and, starting with a cotillon shortly before twelve o'clock, danced until nightfall. After supper we drove to Peshtigo, cleared out the large attic of the boarding-house, and continued our festivities until after seven o'clock the following morning.

In these days the charivari also was a recognized institution, and many a groom faced the ordeal of noise made by beating circular saws suspended on cords or ropes. The only escape from the terrific clanging was to "treat" the crowd in one way or another. Many times I was appealed to by the prospective bridegroom who sought a way of escaping from the ear-splitting serenade. The most enjoyable form of diversion, however, was an excursion to a neighboring village on the bay by steamer. More than once I took the entire community, men, women, and children, on board one or more vessels and set out on expeditions of this kind.

CHAPTER XII

*Scarcity of politicians in early lumbering settlements — The Con-
gressional Globe — Early recollections of politics — Distributing
ballots in Chicago in 1856 — Experiences as supervisor and
justice of the peace — An Indian wedding — Campaign of
1860 — Beginning of the Civil War — Furnishing recruits —
Assassination of Lincoln — Fear of Indian massacre.*

IN enumerating the professions or avocations not represented in our lumbering communities along Green
Bay before the middle of the last century — and which
we were able to do without — I might have added politicians. There was none of the machinery of elections, no
voting, no local offices to be filled, no contests to be decided, and consequently no fervent campaigning or discussion of popular rights. In the absence of township or
city organization the superintendent or "boss" was supreme, although his position brought him nothing but
responsibilities, a condition which suited our purposes
much better, I have no doubt, than an elaborate system
of local government. With reference to the larger questions of national polity we were in a situation of splendid
isolation. The only matters that occupied our attention
were those of our immediate environment, and they had
to do exclusively with lumber.

My own interests, however, extended beyond this
restricted field; and I was one of the few, I dare say, who
reached out to the broader horizon of politics. This
could be accomplished through the medium of the *Congressional Globe*, for which I subscribed in the fifties, which

served the purpose of the *Congressional Record* and published a detailed account of the activities of the national legislature. It was printed by Judge Blair, one of whose sons, Francis, a general in the Civil War, subsequently became a candidate for Vice-President with Seymour, and another, Montgomery, was Lincoln's Postmaster-General. In the logging camps in the forest at times and at the mills I was able through the columns of the *Globe* to follow the progress of legislative events; and not a few times, with the information so obtained, discomfited in the course of political argument men from Milwaukee, Chicago, and other cities who assumed that a knowledge of national affairs had not percolated to the out-of-the-way places in the northern forests.

One incident in this connection stands out with peculiar distinctness. Horatio Seymour, who was elected governor of New York in 1862, came to Escanaba in the spring of 1861 and loitered there for a week or more, remaining incognito for political reasons. On his way south he stopped at Marinette, where he was to board the "Queen City" for Green Bay. For six hours we discussed political matters in my office at the mill. He held to the pacific view that the cotton states should be permitted to secede if they wished to do so and that they would return to the Union of their own volition. This I met with the argument that the same rule could be applied to counties wishing to withdraw from states and townships wishing to withdraw from counties, a course that would obviously lead to chaos. None the less the time passed pleasantly and when the boat had taken on her cargo Seymour embarked. At Green Bay, it appeared, he was to have met Judge Lord of St. Louis and a prominent politician from the South who inadvertently disclosed the purpose of his visit while playing a game of cards. Seymour went on to Milwaukee, where his presence was discovered, and made a short and noncommittal speech on the question of secession. On this, as on other occasions, my familiarity with debates in Congress enabled me to discuss intelligently the various aspects of public problems.

My earliest introduction to politics came when I was a youth in Bangor. Before that I had seen as a small boy something of the excitement which attended the campaigns and elections in New Brunswick,— very often marked by hostilities between the Orangemen and the Catholics,— when my elders were importuned to cast their "plumpers," whole votes as distinguished from fractional votes, for one or the other of the rival candidates. But it was in Maine that the responsibilities of citizenship were first held up to me. While driving across the bridge with the sister of Mrs. March, whose husband was a partner of Mr. Sinclair, we saw in the public square a floating banner inscribed with the names of Polk and Dallas, presidential and vice-presidential candidates on the Democratic ticket. "Isaac," said my companion, who had acted to some extent as my teacher also, "if I had anything to do with politics, I would be a Whig. I certainly wouldn't be one of those old loco-focos."

Whether or not I acted upon her advice, I followed that course. The men with whom I had been associated were Whigs, the sailors on the lakes, as I have said, were Whigs, and it was but natural in this environment that I should become a Whig also. Before I attained voting age, however, the party became defunct and was succeeded by the Republican party, to which I have given my support from the time of its organization down to the present day. The only part I played in the affairs of the

Whig party was that of an ardently interested onlooker during the election of President Taylor in 1848, when I was nineteen years old.

One of my earliest recollections of a political event in the Middle West is of a gathering in the courthouse square in Milwaukee in 1847, when Governor Dodge, of the Territory of Wisconsin, delivered an address. Shaking with malaria,— "ague-and-chill" fever, as it was more commonly called,— I sat on the ground with my back against an oak tree on the outskirts of the crowd, a melancholy figure, while the governor conveyed his message, whatever it might have been, to the populace. If he had any political principles to expound, they were lost on me.

The first service I rendered the Republican party was to "peddle" tickets for Fremont and Dayton, at the City Hall in Chicago, on November 3, 1856. At this time I was associated with Holt and Mason, for whom I logged by contract at Masonville, and happened to come to Chicago on a business trip with Mr. Holt at the time of the national election. He was an ardent Republican and induced me, although I was unable to vote, to render such service as I could by distributing ballots. The day was cold, and the sleet and snow whipped by a gale from the lake had turned the streets of Chicago into a dismal area of mud. But I stuck to my post all day, hailing voters and urging the claims of Fremont.

In Marinette, which was then included in the territory of Oconto County, by reason of my position in the industrial life of the community, I was singled out for political responsibilities almost as soon as the town emerged from the camp stage of its development. In 1859, the year after the mill of the N. Ludington Company came under my charge, I was elected supervisor of the town, an office which I held for fifteen years. For fourteen years, also, as justice of the peace, I did more than my share to settle petty disturbances, patch up disagreements, officiate at weddings, and otherwise keep the life of the community running smoothly.

In the latter capacity, however, I tried but few cases and accomplished much more as a peacemaker than as a magistrate. In most instances the litigants could be persuaded to settle their differences amicably. In two cases I awarded damages of twenty-five dollars, which were increased to fifty dollars when appeal was taken to the Circuit Court by the disgruntled party.

Serious cases, fortunately, we did not have, but some of them were what might be described as stubborn. One in particular arose over a half-barrel of pickles worth about four dollars. Two residents of Marinette who had been good friends for years became glowering enemies, engaged attorneys, to whom they paid ten dollars each, and settled down defiantly to fight to the last ditch until they had secured justice — or vengeance, all to determine merely who owned and who did not own the pickles. When the case was brought before me I continued it for a week, hoping that time would subdue the enmity, but when it had elapsed there was no cooling of belligerent spirits. They appeared in court with their counsel prepared to argue the case.

Thereupon I laid my magisterial dignity, or whatever I had of it, aside and led the two principals into a corner. "The pickles," I said, "cost four dollars. You have each paid a lawyer ten dollars, lost three or four days of time, and spoiled your peace of mind. When it is all over neither of you will have any satisfaction and both of you will have more expenses. Why go to all this trouble?"

The two litigants began to see the situation in a different light. Their defiance melted, they shook hands and dismissed the lawyers, and became the good friends they were before. Technically speaking this might not have been administering justice, but it was the course I chose to follow.

As justice of the peace it also became my duty to officiate at more than a score of weddings, most of which were of my own making. Many of the young men who could wield axes in the forest masterfully, drive logs in the turbulent river, and saw lumber were more or less inarticulate when it came to wooing and needed impetus of one kind or another to encourage them to take the plunge. I adopted the method of suggesting adroitly to the man and woman that the one was very much interested in the other and kept the interest of the young people alive, if necessary, by constant reiteration. Sooner or later this inspired confidence, the shyness was overcome, and the match was made.

Not all of these weddings, however, were of an idyllic sort. One day I was summoned to the house of a trapper who, following a rather primitive practice not unusual at the time, had for twenty years lived with an Indian woman of the Menominee tribe. During all these years they had not regarded a marriage ceremony as a necessity, but the advantage of it was brought home to them when the government required a marriage certificate as a condition precedent for the payment of five dollars a month to the wives of men who had enlisted. The trapper was drafted and to insure the payment of the money to his squaw they sent for me to perform the civil ceremony.

The woman in her feminine way looked forward to the event with elation. She appeared smiling radiantly, with her face shining, almost dripping with sturgeon oil, the Indian idea of cosmetics, and decked out in the glaring finery that stirred her aboriginal sense of beauty. The groom was less radiant, regarding the affair as an unavoidable bother. I did my best to enter into the spirit of the occasion from the woman's point of view, made the ceremony as impressive as possible, joined their hands with great gravity, and pronounced them man and wife.

"Now," said the groom when I had finished, glowering at the smiling bride, "I hope to heaven you're satisfied!"

During the campaign of 1860, when Lincoln was a candidate for the first time, I was again in Chicago and did not vote, but took an active part in the canvass in Wisconsin. These were days of stress and storm and the shadow of war already seemed to be upon us. If we had escaped the turmoil of politics up to this time it was only to have it thrust upon us in more than full measure with the discussion over the slave question and other problems that threatened the disruption of the nation. The Republicans were, of course, for Lincoln and there were a number of Douglas Democrats who were opposed to secession and were not altogether sympathetic with the Southern point of view. But there was also among the laboring men a large element of "copperheads," constituting more than half the Democratic voters, who were bitter in their antagonism toward the administration and rejoiced whenever a Confederate victory was proclaimed. They cultivated very zealously the foolish fear that if the slaves were liberated they would overrun the North and demoralize the labor market.

When the gathering storm broke, shortly after President Lincoln's election, the task of making preparation for it overshadowed all other activity, and much of my

time was given up to filling our quota of troops. On
March 4, 1862, Colonel Balcolm, of Oconto, went to Washington and offered the President a regiment of soldiers
of which, according to the plans we had made, he was to
be colonel and I lieutenant-colonel. The organization
was to be one of lumbermen, who, after a winter in the
woods, were in the best possible physical condition to undergo the vicissitudes of a military campaign except for
the lack of training. It would be, we contemplated, one
of the "crack" regiments of the army. The plans, however, were never carried out nor our ambitions achieved.
The government declined the offer on the ground that
it had all the men it wanted at the time and was without
guns to equip more.

In September, 1862, a draft was ordered and my name
appeared in the list. I was anxious to go to the front, but
the other members of the N. Ludington Company contended that I would be of far greater service to the country
by remaining where I was, as there was no one else available to take charge of the mill and keep the business upon
which a large part of the community depended for a living, going. I therefore went to Green Bay and secured
my release by purchase, paying at the same time for the
release of several of the men whose services at the mill
could not be dispensed with.

In the meantime I did what I could to encourage en-
listment. In 1863, when a ninety-day company was organized, I induced thirteen men to join by paying them,
in addition to the thirteen dollars a month they received
from the government, another thirteen dollars; so that
their pay while in service would amount to twenty-six
dollars. Later I induced ten or twelve other men to en-
roll by offering a similar bonus. I also took the initiative

in having the county board adopt a resolution to pay one hundred and twenty dollars to every man that enlisted and was credited to Oconto County. In other ways, too, there was aid to be extended. A carpenter, by way of illustration, said he would go to the front if he could dispose of his tools; and I paid him fifty dollars for them, though they were scarcely worth ten.

The last call for recruits came while I was on my way to Washington to attend the inauguration of Lincoln the second time. Word was sent to me at Green Bay and I immediately made arrangements for supplying fourteen men, contributing $2,200 to that end, and telegraphed to the New York Company suggesting that they subscribe a similar amount. These men did not proceed farther than Madison when peace was declared, and a part of the money we had contributed was repaid in town and county orders reduced in value to thirty cents on the dollar. Although very sparsely populated, Oconto County supplied two companies during the war. Brown County, in which Green Bay is situated, contributed more officers than men during the first two years — a comparison not unfavorable to us.

The news of Lincoln's assassination on April 14, 1865, was brought to us by a boat, the captain of which sent me a note as soon as he had dropped anchor at the mouth of the harbor. It was Sunday morning. My buggy was at the door and I was about to drive to church with my wife when a man rode up with the brief message that the President had been shot by John Wilkes Booth at Ford's Theater in Washington.

Even under the shadow of this national catastrophe the hostility of the misguided "copperheads" was not altogether suppressed. As I turned to read the captain's

note to a group of persons that had gathered about me,
one of them, an employee at the mill, clapped his hands
in manifestation of his approval of the murder and turning
to the others said: "Let's go over to Jack's saloon and
get a drink." For the moment I could scarcely control
my indignation, and I told him in no uncertain terms that
the earth would be well rid of him and his kind. By way
of retribution, perhaps, for the offensive remark, the arm
of the man who made it was blown off by an exploding
cannon on July 4 of the same year, an accident over which,
I must confess, I felt little regret. The doleful message
announcing the assassination of Lincoln was sent down
to the minister, who read it to the congregation; and even
in this far distant village, despite the exultation of the
"copperheads," the gloom of mourning fell. I hope I may
never see the turmoil and the bitterness of those days
again.

There was one other occasion during this period when
the villages along Green Bay and throughout Wisconsin
generally were stirred to the pitch of military excitement
and made elaborate preparations for defense. This was
in 1862. An Indian massacre at New Ulm, Minnesota,
had awakened the fear of a general uprising of the savages
which spread like a prairie fire, increasing in intensity as
it progressed. Soon the obsession assumed the proportions
of a panic. Everywhere throughout the state people on
isolated farms or in forest camps congregated around the
nearest villages for protection. Even in the vicinity of
Milwaukee men, women, and children hastened to the
city and for several days the streets were congested with
refugees encamped there.

The danger was remote. It was preposterous to assume
that a band of Indians, even though considerable in num-

bers, could traverse a wilderness of several hundred miles and raid cities and towns. Nevertheless, the fear was genuine though groundless. In Marinette the Indians and half-breeds were as panic-stricken as the white people, and to meet the situation and prevent the workmen at the mills from deserting their posts we perfected a military organization and commissioned Dr. Hall and one or two others to go to Madison to obtain a hundred Belgian rifles, a part of the stock Fremont had purchased in Europe at the outbreak of the war. These weapons were all but useless, but they served our purpose as they restored the confidence of the people in their ability to defend themselves. The company elected me captain and, with the aid of Hardy's tactics, which I studied assiduously, I drilled the men for more than a month. At the end of that time the panic had abated and normal conditions were restored.

CHAPTER XIII

Business revival after panic and Civil War — Development of Menominee River region and creation of boom company — William B. Ogden and Samuel J. Tilden — I become manager of Peshtigo Company — Erection of woodenware manufacturing plant — Establishment of barge lines for transporting lumber — Origin of signal for tows — Construction of Sturgeon Bay Canal — Adoption of cedar for railroad ties.

TOWARD the close of the war, even before peace had been actually declared, the country began slowly to shake off the lethargy from which it had not recovered altogether since the panic of 1857. Industry revived, the current of trade began to move again, and a period of development, which was to endure for several years, was soon under way. The effect of the revival upon the lumber industry was most pronounced. The average price, which had been only twelve dollars a thousand up to 1863, reached twenty-four dollars before the end of the following year.

The change marked the beginning of a tremendous development of the Menominee River region, the production of which was to mount upward within less than a score of years from one hundred million to approximately seven hundred million feet. More mills were erected, older mills were enlarged, and on the lower reaches of the river and along the bay shore the lumber area steadily expanded. Operations in the forests above were extended with proportionate rapidity. This necessitated the creation of a central organization to handle the enormous number of

161

logs driven down the stream and distribute them among the numerous manufacturing plants and resulted in the incorporation of the Menominee River Manufacturing Company, afterward called the Menominee River Boom Company.

In 1865 I had built piers in the river to facilitate the handling of timber, but these proved to be inadequate for the growing requirements and during the following year a freshet swept several million feet of logs out into the bay. This awakened the mill owners to the necessity of concerted action, and the establishment of the boom, which had for its prototype the Oldtown boom on the Penobscot, constructed and managed by Jefferson Sinclair, followed soon after.

This placed additional responsibilities upon my shoulders. There was no one else among the mill owners who had had practical experience in this kind of work, in which I had learned many valuable lessons from Mr. Sinclair and the lumbermen of Maine, and I was accordingly made president of the concern, an office which I still hold, and given full direction of its affairs. It was no small task. To secure the necessary flow of water and regulate the swift current of the river, forty dams were built on the main stream and its tributaries, some of which supply power for traction, lighting, and manufacturing to-day. These were of the gravity type with a broad sloping base. In constructing them we were without the advice of engineers and the advantages of modern mechanical contrivances and materials, but they have stood the test of a half-century. On the Peshtigo River I built twenty-seven more dams, making sixty-seven in all — a record in which I take some pride.

The Menominee River Boom Company is no longer the important institution it was in the halcyon days of lumbering. The millions of feet of pine and hemlock logs, which sometimes extended from bank to bank for miles along the stream, have dwindled to less than one-tenth of the original number, as the forests have been stripped and the huge straight trunks free of limbs have given way to small knotted timber, but the system remains the same.

These were days of large industrial enterprise and men of great capacity and breadth of view were required to encompass and make the most of the opportunities that began to appear upon the brightening horizon. And such men were forthcoming. Some of them, it seems, were endowed with almost prophetic vision and yet were sufficiently trained in the school of experience to progress with safe and sure steps toward the attainment of the dimly discernible ideals that have since been realized. Many of these men it was my good fortune, by reason of the position I held, to be associated with and to know.

Towering above all of them physically as well as mentally, in energy, breadth of vision, and masterful enterprise, was William B. Ogden, the first mayor of Chicago. For ten years I was closely associated with him in business and saw much of him at his home in Chicago and later on in New York. During that time I had ample time to judge of him in an environment of business men. To my mind he was one of the dominating figures of the Middle West during this period and had as much if not more to do with its development than any other man.

He was moderate, almost abstemious, in his habits. He worked eighteen hours out of the twenty-four, planning his schemes of constructive enterprise and reviewing matters submitted to him for final decision. Only a small part of the undertakings he had projected were carried out, but even these gave him place as a man of very large business affairs. He was one of the pioneers who built the railroad from Galena to Chicago. He also built the Northwestern Railroad from Chicago to Green Bay and was president of and a large stockholder in the company. In Chicago and elsewhere his enterprises were almost without number, and his activities as agent of wealthy capitalists in the United States and abroad covered a wide field.

When the panic of 1857 came, Mr. Ogden had outstanding paper to the amount of $1,500,000, a much larger sum according to the scale of operations at that time than it appears measured by present standards. When he went to New York to arrange matters to tide himself over the crisis he engaged Samuel J. Tilden as his attorney. Subsequently the two men became very fast friends and Tilden was made a director in the Northwestern Railroad Company. In such esteem was Mr. Ogden held in Chicago that upon his return from this trip he was greeted by bonfires all over the city.

In the fires of 1871, at Chicago and Peshtigo, he lost upward of five million dollars, possibly twice or thrice that sum. When the disaster overtook him two of his clients, one a wealthy man in New York, another in England, wrote to his brother, Mahlon Ogden, who was in charge of his real estate operations, directing him to sell out their holdings and devote the proceeds to the liquidation of Mr. Ogden's debts. By this display of friendship Mr. Ogden was deeply touched, and from that time until his death in 1878 the portraits of his two benefactors, who, as it happened, were not called upon to make the sacrifice they proposed, hung in his house. Despite the losses he suffered, he left a large estate.

In the autumn of 1864 Mr. Ogden and Mr. Tilden, who were returning from an inspection of their mines

WILLIAM B. OGDEN .

in the Lake Superior copper district, stopped at Marinette on their way to Chicago and were my guests for thirty-six hours. The national campaign was then in full swing. Both Mr. Ogden and Mr. Tilden were of the Democratic faith, although they were in favor of the preservation of the Union and upheld the principle of protection, and had before leaving Chicago played a conspicuous part in the nomination of George B. McLellan on the Democratic ticket. They told me at the time that the platform upon which McLellan ran was prepared in Mr. Ogden's library. It was the best, Mr. Tilden said, that Vallandigham's wing of the party, the "copperheads," would accept. I gave Mr. Tilden a copy of the Green Bay *Advocate* containing a copy of McLellan's letter of acceptance, and after reading it he observed that McLellan had added the soldiers' plank in accordance with a suggestion he had made to him to "tune it up some."

A few years later I had occasion to go to New York several times on business matters, and on one of these visits, while stopping with Mr. Ogden at his home, an imposing residence on the Harlem River just above the aqueduct bridge, made the suggestion that Tilden, who had then been governor of New York, was the strongest candidate the Democrats could select for President. The same idea must have been lurking in Mr. Ogden's mind, although I had never heard it expressed before, for, when I made the remark, his face brightened.

"Stephenson," he said eagerly "will you support him?"

"Oh, no!" I replied. "I am a Republican."

In 1876 Tilden was nominated and, it is very generally admitted, was elected, although counted out. From patriotic motives, it was said at the time, he preferred to make no contest rather than stir up serious trouble.

From Marinette Mr. Ogden and Mr. Tilden went to Peshtigo, where the former had a large lumbering establishment. Using this as a nucleus it was his purpose to erect a large plant for the manufacture of woodenware and other products, but he encountered serious difficulty in the lack of a manager in whom he had confidence to take charge of these operations. For four years, since I had first met him in 1863, he had tried to induce me to take part in the enterprise. At length, in July, 1867, I bought fifty thousand dollars worth of stock and became vice-president and general manager of the Peshtigo Company.

We began operations on a large scale. The fifty thousand acres of timber lands which the company had when I assumed direction of its affairs were increased to one hundred and twenty-five thousand in the course of the next five or six years. In addition to the water-mill at the village of Peshtigo we erected at the mouth of the river a steam mill, the largest and most complete establishment of its kind in the West. The two had a combined capacity of from fifty to sixty million feet of lumber a year, and on the first day of the operation of the new plant the men, in a working day of eleven hours and using selected logs and putting forth their best efforts, sawed approximately 350,000 feet of lumber and 53,000 lath, a record for that time.

In 1868 we began the erection of a factory for the manufacture of wooden pails. There were two of these already in Wisconsin, one at Two Rivers, owned by Mann Brothers, and another at Menasha, owned by E. D. Smith, whom we induced to take an interest in our enterprise. We also entered upon the manufacture of broom handles and clothes pins under the direction of a man, whom we brought from New Hampshire, reputed to be the most skillful in the country in this branch of industry. The magnitude of our operations may be gathered from the fact that at one time we had in the yards drying two and one-half million feet of basswood boards to be made into broom handles. In addition we built twenty drying-houses, two large warehouses,— one of them three hundred feet long and five stories in height,— and smaller buildings. At Chicago we maintained a large lumber yard, and used for the storage of woodenware the old sugar refinery on North Point. Mr. Ogden also contemplated the establishment of a large tannery and took up negotiations with one of the largest firms in New England for that purpose, but before the plan could be carried out the great fire in 1871 intervened.

Our work, however, consisted of much more than the erection of buildings. The problem of transportation still confronted us. It was necessary for us to bring our manufactured products to the bay from Peshtigo, a distance of seven miles, to construct a harbor where vessels could be loaded, and to ship it thence to the market at Chicago. This involved many difficult problems.

A railroad from the village to Green Bay, equipped with locomotives which we obtained from the Northwestern Railroad and transported on scows, provided the first link. At the mouth of the Peshtigo River a private harbor was made by driving piles out to deep water and filling in the intervening spaces with slabs and edgings. This plan proved so successful that it attracted the attention of the government engineers who for three or four years came to make an annual inspection; and, becoming convinced finally of the value of the methods we had followed, adopted them for the construction of many of the piers and harbors at lumber ports.

The transportation of the lumber and other commodities to Chicago presented greater difficulties. The railroad did not extend beyond Green Bay city and, besides, the freight charges were prohibitive. On the other hand, the cost of carrying lumber on ships was excessive. To reduce this item of expense it occurred to me to use barges, a decided innovation, as it was thought impossible up to this time to tow these craft on the rough waters of Lake Michigan. We purchased two tugs: the "Reindeer," which was brought from New York by way of Oswego, and the "Admiral Porter," a larger vessel, which came through Canada by way of the Welland Canal. Subsequently we disposed of the "Porter" because it was not strong enough for our purposes, trading it for a larger boat.

The barges we had built at the shipyard at Trenton, near Detroit. There were six in all, three with a capacity of one million feet of lumber each and three that carried half this amount. These we proposed to tow in pairs. While one of the larger and one of the smaller vessels were in transit, another pair was at Chicago unloading and another at Peshtigo taking on cargo. From the very outset the plan worked successfully. Thus was established the first barge line on Lake Michigan.

Having accomplished this much, we decided to enlarge the tows and I went to Cleveland, Detroit, and Bay City to purchase more barges to avoid the loss of time required to build them; but there were none suitable for our purposes. At this time there was only one barge line, a very small one, on the lower lakes running from Bay City to Cleveland. The captain of the tug "Prindiville," — heralded abroad as the best vessel of its kind in these waters,— who had charge of the line, contended that barges could not be successfully towed on Lake Michigan.

When he left Bay City, he said, he encountered rough water for a distance of only fifty miles and, if the wind were unfavorable, he turned back. From the mouth of the river to Cleveland he was exposed to rough weather for another fifty miles. His experiences with these short stretches convinced him that towing on the open lake where contrary winds and storms prevailed was an impossible feat. He was somewhat taken aback when I informed him not only that it could be done but that we were actually doing it successfully.

Our example was soon followed by others. After we had operated our barges from Peshtigo to Chicago for two years, four companies on the Menominee, including the N. Ludington Company, which was still under my direction, adopted the plan and we purchased the barge line operated by Theisen, Filer and Robinson, of Manistique, Michigan. Extensive additions were made to this equipment and in two or three years we had fifteen barges in operation towing five at a time. We instituted another innovation on the Menominee by designing the tug "Parrot" for the use of slabs as fuel. On this item alone we effected a saving of five thousand dollars a year. The vessel carried one hundred cords of this wood, which was then inexpensive, sufficient to make the round trip from Marinette to Chicago.

The establishment of the barge lines raised the problem of signaling passing vessels, especially during the night or in foggy weather when there was danger of colliding with the tow. The usual signal of one whistle gave warning of the approach of the tug, but not of the barges behind. A number of years later, in 1884, when I was a member of the House of Representatives, I filed with the Secretary of the Treasury a petition recommending the adoption of a special signal for a tow. Of the nine supervising inspectors of the Bureau of Navigation four were in favor of the proposal and five opposed to it. I thereupon took up the question directly with Judge Folger, then Secretary, explaining to him the conditions, and pointing out the danger to navigation not only from our own barges but from the tows of logs which were brought from Canada in booms. Fortunately he had been on Lake Michigan the year before and, while on his way from Chicago to Sturgeon Bay on the revenue cutter "Andy Johnson," had met our tow. He easily understood the situation and it was not difficult to win him over to my position.

I proposed a signal of three whistles at short intervals. He issued the order despite the disagreement among the inspectors, and it was adopted. It has always been the occasion of much satisfaction to me, not only that my recommendation was followed, but that the signal is used to-day in all waters under the jurisdiction of the United States and has, possibly, obviated many dangers and saved many lives.

The progress we made in the improvisation of new methods and the reduction of the cost of transportation has since dropped into the background, and these achievements are largely only of historical interest. With the advent of the big steel freighters, the development of railroads, and the establishment of important terminals, the entire problem has been transformed and even the old wooden vessels are disappearing. At the time, however, what we did was of great value not only to ourselves but to others and perhaps it was but a step in the direction of all that since has been attained.

Another important improvement in connection with water transportation to and from Green Bay which, though accomplished in later years, I may mention here, was the construction of the Sturgeon Bay Canal, an artificial channel across the peninsula jutting out into Lake Michigan from the northeastern part of Wisconsin. Before the completion of this waterway it was necessary for vessels from Green Bay ports to make a wide detour around the barrier by way of Death's Door, the rocky passage between the islands at the northern extremity.

The project of building a canal across the narrow neck of land at Sturgeon Bay called the portage had been under discussion for some years, but nothing was done until the Peshtigo Company took the initiative in the formation of a corporation to undertake the work of construction. At the outset obstacles were encountered. The general rate of interest on money was ten per cent. People who were expected to take an interest in the completion of the improvement assumed an attitude of indifference and declined to contribute to the fund we attempted to raise for a preliminary survey. In Green Bay, the city which was to be most benefited by it, the only subscription we obtained was five dollars from one of the prominent lumbermen.

Nevertheless a preliminary survey was made, largely through my efforts and at my expense, but the route contemplated was abandoned because of the discovery of a ledge of rock at the eleven-foot level, an insuperable obstacle because the use of dynamite for under-water blasting was unknown at the time. Later I succeeded in having the government engineers make another survey for a route a mile and a half in length. This was adopted, a grant of two hundred thousand acres of land, odd sections lying for the most part in Marinette County, was authorized and the company began work in the early seventies.

General Strong, secretary of the Peshtigo Company, Mr. Ogden, Jesse Spalding, and myself had charge of the enterprise; but the actual direction of the affairs of the corporation fell largely to me, as the others were without the practical knowledge needed for work of this kind.

About midway in the work of excavation we encountered a ridge, thirty feet above water level, covered with a heavy growth of timber. In removing this we came upon a cedar tree, fourteen inches in diameter at the butt, buried under forty-three feet of earth. How long it had been there is, of course, a matter of speculation. But in view of the depth of the soil above it and the size of the trees that had taken root there it seemed probable that it had been covered for two or three centuries or more. In spite of its great age every branch, even the bark, was perfectly preserved; and so great was the curiosity aroused over it that we sent sections to various parts of the country for examination, and scientists endeavored to solve the problem of its antiquity.

The discovery confirmed the conclusion I had reached several years before: that cedar resisted decay much more effectively than other woods of the northern region. While making repairs on the company's railroad from the village of Peshtigo to the bay I found that a cedar tie, which had been used inadvertently, was in a much better state of preservation than others adjoining it, although they had all been laid at the same time. This gave me the clue that was borne out by the cedar tree unearthed in digging the canal, and I proposed to Mr. Ogden and other railroad men that cedar, which was of little value at the time for other purposes, be used for ties. My suggestion met with opposition. Mr. Ogden contended that it was too soft, but eventually he yielded to my judgment, others followed

our example, and in time the cedar tie became one of the
staple products of all northern lumbering establishments.

The canal was carried through to completion as expeditiously and economically as any work ever undertaken under like conditions; harbors were constructed
and the waterway was opened to traffic in 1873. The two
hundred thousand acres of land granted the company
was at the time of little value. Most of it was swampy
or boggy and it had been for the most part stripped of
timber. We disposed of it at two auctions, at one of
which we sold 77,000 acres for $38,000. At present the
tract would be worth millions, but no one foresaw the
agricultural development that was to follow. In 1893
the canal was purchased by the government for $103,000.

CHAPTER XIV

*Difficulties at Peshtigo — Extension of the Northwestern Railroad
northward from Green Bay — Forest fires — The great fire of
1871 — Destruction of Peshtigo with loss of eleven hundred lives
— Relief work — Antics of the fire — Horrors of the holocaust
— Conflagration at Chicago — Distributing supplies and rebuilding of village — Resumption of lumbering — Difficulties
of reconstruction.*

U P to the autumn of 1871 the huge outlay we had
made at Peshtigo on the construction of factories
and mills had brought us no return. The market
for woodenware appeared to be glutted and in some instances we were forced to sell our product at a loss. Moreover, the expenses of handling, transporting, and storing,
in spite of the reductions we had made by the use of barges,
were still excessive.

To improve these conditions our efforts had been directed toward securing the extension of the Northwestern
Railroad from the city of Green Bay to the Menominee.
Mr. Ogden, so long as he remained on the directorate,
was unwilling to use his influence in furthering this plan
for fear his motive might be misinterpreted as a desire to
advance his own interests at Peshtigo. The burden, therefore, fell principally upon me, and I made a number of
trips to New York, not to speak of many to Chicago, to
confer with the railroad officials and lay the case before
them.

Finally we succeeded, two years after Mr. Ogden had
retired from the directorate. In 1871 the railroad company

began to extend its line northward, giving us the prospect of a much-needed outlet which would enable us to distribute our products directly throughout the West without the necessity of reshipment at Chicago. In other respects also the outlook brightened and we were confident that we had reached a point at which we could make a profit on our operations.

But in our efforts to better our position we unwittingly paved the way for disaster. The summer and autumn of 1871 were unusually dry and the forests and brush were reduced to tinder. To make conditions worse, the wind blew almost continuously for day after day from the southwest. When work on the railroad was begun fires were started to clear the right of way. The contractors carelessly allowed these to spread and they ran through the country with startling rapidity, feeding on the dry forests. In some instances even the marshes and bogs were burned to a depth of four feet.

For five weeks before October 8 we had fought small fires in the woods in the vicinity of Peshtigo and the air was so murky with smoke that people went about on the streets with red and watering eyes. On the afternoon of Saturday, October 7, I drove from Marinette to the village of Peshtigo and went down to the harbor where the steam sawmill was situated. On my return on the evening of the same day tongues of flame darting through the woods were visible from the roadway. These were the forerunners of the great disaster.

The sporadic fires seemed only to kindle the forest and bring it to the point of inflammability to be consumed later. On the night of Sunday, October 8, about nine o'clock, the flames, fanned by a high wind, leaped into a fury and sweeping in a northeasterly direction over a path twelve miles wide encompassed the village of Peshtigo, transformed it into a smoking waste and took toll of its people to the number of eleven hundred. Gathered into a tornado of fire they rushed on with incredible rapidity, vaulted the river, and died out only when they reached the impassable barrier of water which confronted them on the shore of Green Bay, north of Menominee.

In the blackened wake every form of life was obliterated. In many instances tiny heaps of white ashes marked the places where men, women, and children had fallen; and where the forest had been, gaunt disfigured tree trunks stood like sentinels of death under the low-hanging pall of smoke.

In Peshtigo a number of people took refuge in the river and stood for an hour or more in the water, all but blinded and suffocated by the intense heat and smoke, while the fiery turmoil raged on all sides of them. But most of the population had been overtaken in their houses or on the streets by the sudden outburst and were numbered among the missing. Every house was gone and only twisted ruins marked the places where the factory, mills, the supply store, and other buildings had been. Even a mile of our railroad had been burned and the locomotive and cars were a tangled mass of iron. The loss was complete.

In Marinette we were struggling with another fire which broke out an hour later and burned everything from the middle to the lower end of the city. The path of the flames which had devastated Peshtigo lay just to the north. Between the two we struggled all night in the blinding smoke and intense heat, not knowing how soon the seething fringes of fire would close in upon us. The air itself was livid and seemed to burst into sheets of flame, and the withering maelstrom spat fiery tongues that consumed whatever they touched. In some places they overleaped piles of dry brush which a spark would have ignited, yet burned the grass to within ten feet of them. The fire appeared to break out spontaneously in pockets or dart forward in tortuous flashes instead of progressing with uniform pace, which accounted for the strange contrasts it left in its ruined wake. None the less its path from Peshtigo to the bay was clearly marked and varied little in width for the entire distance.

Many persons in Menominee and Marinette, abandoning their homes when they realized the fury of the raging conflagration, went aboard a steamer which put out into the bay. Many others, employees of the mill quartered in the big boarding-house not far away, and women and children, not knowing where to turn, took refuge with us and huddled in silent fright in my house and barns wherever they could find room. Ten or fifteen men in my garden fought back the creeping flames on the edge of the path of the fiery blast which had swept upward from Peshtigo.

When the danger was greatest my brother-in-law, whose house and barn were not more than three hundred feet away from my own, ran over to tell me that they were burning. The buildings would have been consumed had it not been for one of the antics of the fire. I watched the sheet of flame sweep toward them, but when it came to the house it merely scorched one end and stopped and died out. In my own house my family had made ready to go to the river a short distance away at the moment I gave the signal.

As is usual in such crises, most of the people in a panic of fear were as helpless as children; and even under the shadow of the appalling destruction that was being wrought some of the incidents that occurred at this time were of the most ludicrous character. Two hired girls at my house were aiding the men fighting the fire, and one of them I instructed to watch over some corn which had been shocked and was standing in the rear of the garden. Her chief interest, however, was a little patch of cabbages of her own growing. I discovered that she watched solicitously over the cabbage patch and kept it drenched with water, although it could not burn. But the inflammable corn was left to its fate. It required very violent and peremptory language to bring the poor woman's wits back to her.

In the midst of our own dangers we were unaware of the fate of Peshtigo. Many of us kept our vigil until dawn without rest or respite until the roaring flames had passed and the embers had been extinguished. In the morning, not long after I had made a survey of the town, I saw coming up the road on horseback through the haze of smoke John Mulligan, an ex-pugilist, whom we had employed as boss of one of our camps at Peshtigo. He used a rope for a halter and his clothes were a shirt and trousers. At the sight of him I began to realize that while we were fighting the fire others had suffered, perhaps, greater disaster.

"Johnny, what is the matter?" I asked in alarm. "I haven't heard from Peshtigo this morning."

"Peshtigo is burned up," was Mulligan's brief reply. "There isn't a picket left in the whole village, and a great many people are dead."

In the face of this greater catastrophe our own troubles were forgotten, and I turned my attention at once to the succor of the stricken village. I directed Mulligan to go across the river to Menominee to find my brothers,—

Robert, one of the owners and superintendent of the Ludington, Wells and Van Schaick Company, and Samuel M. Stephenson, one of the owners and manager of the Kirby Carpenter Company,— and ask them to send men and teams to Peshtigo. In the meantime we made preparations for the care of the injured and refugees. By nightfall we had turned the Dunlap Hotel in Marinette into a hospital in which forty-three patients who had been burned were installed.

On Tuesday morning I drove over to Menominee, while the country was still overhung with a pall of smoke from the smoldering forest, to send out appeals for aid. We were isolated from the rest of the world because of the destruction of the telegraph lines and had not even heard of the great fire which had swept Chicago and laid it in ruins at the same hour that we were battling with the flames. I wrote out five messages to be taken to Green Bay by one of the Northwestern steamers which was to stop at Menominee on its way from Escanaba at noon. One of the messages was addressed to the mayor of Green Bay, one to the mayor of Oshkosh, one to the mayor of Fond du Lac, and one to the mayor of Milwaukee. The fifth was to be sent to Governor Fairchild at Madison. All of them contained information of the disaster and requests for assistance in caring for the injured and survivors.

A man was posted on the dock with the messages who was instructed to let fall a plank when the boat approached, so that it could find its way through the smoke which was still thick on the bay. The telegrams were put on the wire at Green Bay and soon afterward a flood of money and provisions began to come in and doctors and other persons were on their way to aid us. Governor Fairchild was not in Madison at the time, but his wife, without awaiting his return, had a car loaded with provisions started for Green Bay by midnight. The following day the work of rescue was well under way. Donations began to arrive and doctors coming on the boat from Green Bay looked after the burned and injured.

After making arrangements to send out the calls for help, on Tuesday morning I drove over to Peshtigo along the edge of the path the fire had followed. First I sent men with teams into the farming country in the vicinity of the obliterated village to build bridges, repair culverts, and clear the roads of the fallen trees and débris so that communication could be restored and the transportation of food and supplies facilitated. In the progress of their work they came upon an old man named Leach, sitting on a stone smoking his pipe, the picture of desolation and despair. During the two days following the fire he had buried eleven of his children and grandchildren and remained alone with the ruins of his farm about him.

As we worked in the blackened débris and ashes, at every turn we came upon the horrible evidence of the destructive fury of the flames. For more than a week we found bodies or parts of bodies. By noon on Tuesday we had collected and interred one hundred and thirty-nine, some of them whole, some merely ghastly fragments. In many cases, however, there was nothing left of human beings other than a streak of light ashes which would scarcely have filled a thimble. In others the bones as well as the flesh had been consumed and only the teeth remained. The only means of identification were keys, jack-knives, or other metal objects. Sometimes the bodies of the victims lay in groups. Near the factory ten men were discovered lying on their faces within a space of twelve feet, with their hands covering their eyes.

But the effects of the fire were not everywhere the
same. By the side of the streaks of white ashes or charred
remains were bodies that lay almost as they had fallen,
untouched by flame and bearing no evidence of the con-
suming heat, grewsome relics of the frightful holocaust.
On the first day of the rescue work we came upon the bodies
of a Mrs. Tanner and her two children, a boy about three
years old with flaxen hair and a girl five or six years old.
Mrs. Tanner, we discovered afterwards, had put the children to bed and gone down town and had evidently returned to rescue them when the torrent of fire engulfed the
village. The little girl's hand was clasped in hers and
the boy's body lay five or six feet away. Hers was the
only body we found face upward. All the others had
fallen forward, some in crouching positions, apparently
trying to shield their eyes from the awful heat. The
clothes had been burned from the children but their hair
remained untouched, scarcely singed by the flames.

Two days after the grewsome search began we discovered, in a kneeling position with the face resting on the
ground, the body of a man who had been employed on a
street in the rear of the factory. It was clothed in a
gray suit and heavy underwear, and the only evidence
of fire was a spot as large as a man's hand burned through
the coat.

These inexplicable effects of the conflagration, which
seemed to avoid some objects as miraculously as it consumed others, were subsequently made the subject of
close investigation by scientists from various universities; but whether they arrived at any conclusion with
respect to them I do not know. The heat seemed to have
moved in gusts or currents with such irregularity that
in some cases persons escaped who lived not more than

ten feet or more from those who had been reduced to ashes. It was not a matter of intensity alone. In our store were sixty dozens of axes which had run together in an incongruous mass. On a hand fire-engine, called the Black Hawk, heavy iron was melted at the point of the tongue, and two feet away the wood was not charred nor the paint even scorched.

With what agony of despair the victims of the awful catastrophe sought to escape the withering flames may be imagined faintly from the positions in which some of the bodies were found. A young man whom I had intended to make foreman of a camp the following winter had climbed a tree in a small grove near a church. Every day for a week I had driven by within thirty feet of the blackened trunk before I observed the charred corpse, which fell to pieces when it was taken down. Other persons took refuge in wells, where they were smothered, and one body was found in a culvert. Of many victims only traces were discovered and some, I have no doubt, were swallowed up by the obliterating cataclysm of flame as completely as if the earth had opened and engulfed them. Shortly before the fire, for example, we had engaged an expert to establish a system of ditches for the cranberry marshes in the vicinity of the village. He employed seven men, all Scandinavians, and all that was left to mark the fact of their existence was the blades of their shovels.

The work of bringing order out of the chaos left in the wake of the fire, building shelter for the survivors, and distributing supplies for the homeless fell upon me, as manager of the Peshtigo Company. The attention of Mr. Ogden was absorbed by the disaster which overtook Chicago at the same time. He first went to Springfield with a committee from the city to urge General

Palmer, the governor of Illinois, to make arrangements for policing the city, a task which was performed for a time by General Phil Sheridan. Afterward Mr. Ogden came to Peshtigo and remained with me for five weeks. His moral support was of great value to me, but he had little practical knowledge of the kind required by such a situation and I was left to my own resources in directing the work of rehabilitation.

On the Sunday following the fire Governor Fairchild came to Marinette and I met him when the boat landed at noon. It was necessary for me to go to Peshtigo immediately afterward, but I saw him again in the evening and discussed relief arrangements with him. On that day we built the first shanty at Peshtigo with rough boards.

The work of distributing supplies was especially difficult. They came from all parts of the country, even as far away as Vermont, where a minister who had formerly been stationed at Peshtigo gathered together a carload coming with it to Green Bay in person. Relief committees were organized at Peshtigo, Green Bay, and Marinette; but as always happens in cases of this kind, the great problem was to give aid only to those who were in need of it. Taking advantage of the general distress, many worthless persons, the shiftless, the idle and vagrant, lived on the commissary all winter, while the worthy, in many instances, were reluctant to urge their claims or seek assistance and consequently were sometimes overlooked. We did the best we could and gradually conditions were restored to a normal basis. There was no lack of money. The responses to our pleas for aid were ready and generous, and our funds were greater than our needs required, the remnant being turned into the state treasury. Had it not been for the Chicago fire the cash contributions would probably have exceeded one million dollars.

The buildings of the Peshtigo Company situated in she village were, of course, in ashes or ruins, and although we made no attempt to resume operations on the same scale as before it was imperative that the sawmills be started without delay. We were in a helpless plight. All of our oxen and most of our horses, about one hundred and fifty in all, had shared the common fate, and there was not an animal left alive in the entire town. I built sheds and houses, and a temporary supply store of rough boards — which was afterward replaced by the permanent store, still standing, for the construction of which I made a contract in five minutes — and restored the bridge across the river.

In the meantime men were set to work making yokes, sleighs, and wagons, and we added to our stock by purchase. Horses and oxen were bought to take the place of those burned. From the Northwestern Railroad we obtained a locomotive and a mile of rails, which enabled us to transport from the steam mill at the harbor the lumber for rebuilding the town. At the same time there were large quantities of dead and charred timber that had to be sawed without delay to forestall the ravages of worms. We established logging camps and during the ensuing winter hauled something over fifty million feet of lumber. The situation called for rapid and decisive action and comprehensive management. Every day for six weeks I was at Peshtigo directing all these operations, the multiplicity of which may be gathered from the fact that during this period our telegraph bill alone totaled four hundred and ninety dollars.

At Chicago the Peshtigo Company also fared badly. The lumber yard on the lake shore north of the harbor with the offices and buildings was completely destroyed. A new barge called the "Green Bay," which had just been built at Trenton and placed in commission and had carried but one load of lumber to Chicago, was burned at the dock with a loss of thirty-five thousand dollars. Our total losses there were approximately one million dollars.

The second week after the fire the foundry and machine shop at Peshtigo resumed operations. During the winter we built a water-mill on the west side of the river. The sawmill, flourmill, and sash and door factory on the east side were not replaced nor did we take up again the manufacture of woodenware. The industry upon which we had founded our hopes was effectually and permanently snuffed out.

The work of reconstruction had its unexpected difficulties. Instead of clamoring for employment, as might have been expected, many persons, too lazy to work, collected around the commissary and did nothing. Others who had been overwrought by the ordeal through which they passed seemed to have lost their senses and for weeks were of no aid whatever. Under these conditions two of the men upon whom I relied much were Ferdinand Armstrong, foreman of our logging operations, and Tom Burns, a young man who had been assistant in the pail factory. They hired men, went about inspecting the progress of the work, reported to me, and carried out my orders.

The strain I underwent at this time was a severe one and during the following spring, upon the advice of my associates, I took a respite from work for the first time since my arrival in Wisconsin, a dozen years before, and with five of my friends made a trip down the Mississippi River to New Orleans and Mobile.

As an aftermath of the catastrophe which had cost so many lives and so much property, the Peshtigo Company withdrew the subscription of twenty thousand dollars it had agreed to make toward the seventy-five thousand dollars to be paid as a bonus for the extension of the railroad, although I gave individually $3500. If the railroad company were not content with the right of way alone, Mr. Ogden said, he would bring suit to recover damages for the losses we had sustained,— the fire having been directly due to the carelessness of the contractors. This proposition they accepted. The work was pushed to completion and on December 27, 1871, the contractors turned over the road to the directors. Thus, at length, Marinette, after passing through the ordeal of fire and narrowly escaping complete destruction, was placed in direct communication with the outer world, and the days of travel on Green Bay over the ice during the winter and by vessel during the summer were over.

During the following year work was undertaken on the gap that still remained between Marinette and Escanaba. This was done in as haphazard a fashion as the work on the extension from Green Bay. The contractors seemed to have neither credit nor money, and for a time it appeared that the railroad would not be able to comply with the condition upon which the State of Michigan had based its grant of land: the completion of the road by January 1, 1873. In June, 1872, the directors of the Northwestern came to Marinette and I went through with them to Marquette, remaining for three days. Beset with misgivings they asked me if the road would be finished by the end of the year. I told them frankly it would not be half completed by that time because of the inefficiency of the contractors. Thereupon Colonel James H. Howe and other directors proposed that I take up the work, guaranteeing me against loss in addition to the payment of a large salary. This I declined to do.

The task was then turned over to contractors from other railroads, and Marvin Hewitt, who had just become superintendent of the Northwestern, came to Green Bay to obtain horses and equipment to facilitate the work. Every resource was taxed to the utmost. Every influence was brought to bear upon the contractors, and the rails were laid with reckless haste. The road was pushed over hills which afterward had to be cut down and across boggy sink holes that were filled with trees. When the final test came, however, fortune smiled on the railroad. Shortly before the arrival of the commissioners who were to pass upon the work on behalf of the State of Michigan, a period of cold weather set in, and the marshes through which the route lay were frozen solid, making an excellent foundation. A foot of snow generously hid all traces of the half-finished work on the roadbed. On the test run the train was pushed to a speed that would have ended in disaster at any other season of the year. From the car windows the commissioners, surrounded with every possible comfort, gazed upon the snow-covered landscape; and when the journey was completed they pronounced the conditions complied with, and the grant was made. For two years afterward the company was at work cutting down the excessive grades, and making fills in the low places and replacing twisted iron rails.

But the gap was bridged, the railroad now extended from Lake Superior to the south, and the end for which I had labored for ten years was attained.

This was not my last experience with railroads. When the Northwestern built the line from Escanaba to Negaunee and Marquette in the sixties, a piece of work which represented, according to Hewitt, the useless expenditure of at least a million dollars, I had proposed to the directors that they follow the old supply road which had led to my camps on the upper Escanaba River. This, I pointed out, would give them a direct route to the mining region, stimulate logging, and, after the forests had been cleared, provide an outlet for the farms that would inevitably take the place of the wilderness. The plan, although it was rejected, did not fall on altogether deaf ears. Mr. Tilden, who was listening to my portrayal of the development that might be expected in future years, dropped his knife and fork and exclaimed: "What a magnificent conception!" At the time I declared that I would myself build a railroad along the route I proposed if there were no one else to do it. This I did many years later, and the prophecy I made bids fair to be realized.

In 1872 General Phil Sheridan, who was an ardent angler, came up to Peshtigo with Daniel Wells, Governor Ludington, George Walker, of Chicago, General Strong, secretary of the Peshtigo Company, and several others, for a fishing trip. I took charge of the expedition and established a camp for them at the junction of the Peshtigo and Thunder rivers, in the heart of what was then virgin country. Here they remained for seven days, during which time they fished for trout, which abounded in these streams, and abandoned themselves to the pleasure and relaxation of the out-of-doors.

As a precaution I had directed a farmer, John Seymour, who lived several miles away, to be on hand at the camp with his team in case there was any hauling to be done.

Awaiting the arrival of the Northwestern Directors at the mouth of the
Menominee River in 1867

He and General Sheridan, who knew nothing of each other's presence, met face to face in the brush on the banks of the Thunder River while fishing.

"Who are you?" asked General Sheridan, surprised at the sight of a strange face in the wilderness.

"I'm John Seymour," was the reply. "And who might you be?"

"I'm General Sheridan," was the equally frank answer.

"Hell!" said Seymour. "You ain't Little Phil! You couldn't command a hundred thousand men."

Sheridan was more amused at Seymour's scepticism than anyone else and many times afterward recalled the unexpected meeting in the wilderness.

General Sheridan and I became very good friends and he afterwards sent me two army tents as a reminder of this expedition up the Peshtigo River. When I was in Congress he came to see me in the House of Representatives and I visited him frequently at the War Department, and we rehearsed again the incidents of his fishing trip.

CHAPTER XV

Early experiences in politics — Election to the Assembly in 1865 —
Revocation of the Oconto River grant — Candidacy for House of
Representatives — Maneuvers of political leaders — Election to
Congress — Campaign of 1884 in interest of Spooner — Re-election
of Sawyer in 1886 — Withdrawal from political field — Efforts
in behalf of Henry C. Payne — Election of Quarles to Senate.

POLITICALLY as well as industrially the field of
my activities broadened immediately after the Civil
War. I had held local offices, the duties of which
were in many respects but the continuation of those I had
performed as superintendent of logging camps and mills
before the civil organization of the community. From
the building of roads, the carrying out of public improvements, and the regulation of general affairs as manager
of the mill, it was but a short step to membership on the
county board, which had most to do with the expanding
problems of local government. For a time, also, I offi-
ciated as postmaster of Marinette. These things involved
no great sacrifice of time taken in conjunction with my
occupation and I did them as a matter of course, as I
would have done them whether I had held office or not.
But when I was called upon to expand my horizon and
shoulder the obligations of state office, my attention was
diverted from the responsibilities nearer at hand, and for
this reason, the prospect of a political career was by no
means alluring.

In 1865, much against my inclination, I was nominated
a candidate for the Assembly on the Republican ticket

and elected practically without opposition. Although it was the custom of the state legislature to adjourn from Friday until Tuesday when in session, these added duties were very irksome to me because, just at this time, we were doing an extensive business and the several companies of which I had charge were enlarging the scope of their operations in response to the commercial revival following the panic and the war. I returned to Marinette every week during the intervals between sessions, coming as far as Green Bay by train and driving over the ice to Marinette. This added to the inconveniences of ˙public office and it was not long before I arrived at the conclusion that a legislative career did not appeal to me. I declined to run again.

The determination to remain in private life, however, and give my attention to business did not long prevail. In the autumn of 1867 the people of Oconto County became very much incensed over the grant of all the state lands in the county to the Eldred Lumber Company, of which Anson Eldred was the guiding spirit, for the improvement of the Oconto River. Much of the land involved in the grant was swampy, but on portions of it was valuable timber, and the people who were not to derive any benefit from the improvement were naturally of the mind that the resources of the many were being squandered to the advantage of the few. Some of the lands even bordered on the Menominee River. The use of them to improve a stream many miles away aroused a storm of protest, and popular wrath was visited upon the heads of the legislators who had acquiesced in the undertaking.

To block the enterprise, if possible, I was urged to reconsider my decision to retire and to run again. This I at first refused to do. The Democrats had nominated

George Smith, of Oconto, and the Republican candidate was Richard Hubbell, son of Judge Levi Hubbell, of Milwaukee. For four weeks the people of Oconto County— or a large proportion of them—tried to persuade me to change my mind, but I remained firm until three days before the election, which was held on a Tuesday. On the Saturday preceding I telegraphed to George Farnsworth, at Oconto, that I was in the field and would accept the commission if the people desired to tender it to me. On Monday morning I went to Oconto and there met Smith, the Democratic nominee, an old friend. He assured me that I had no chance of election whatever, that my candidacy would divide the Republican strength, and that his success was certain.

To this I said nothing, and I did nothing, but allowed the campaign, brief as it was, to take its course without interference or effort. My only outlay was a barrel of apples which I gave to the men at Marinette when my election was announced. The result was more than satisfactory from my point of view. I was not only elected, but received more votes than Smith and Hubbell together. In Marinette every vote was cast for me but one, and the name on that ballot was so badly written that it could not be deciphered. It might have been Stephenson as well as Smith, but I suggested to the canvassers that Smith ought to have it under the circumstances and it was recorded in his favor.

Somewhat reluctantly I returned to the Assembly While there I succeeded in accomplishing the purpose for which I had been mainly elected. The grant to the Eldred company for the improvement of the Oconto River was revoked and the lands were restored to the state. Afterward they were sold from time to time in small pieces.

These were tumultuous days at Madison. Lobbyists in profusion, especially those in the employ of the railroads, hovered in the shadow of the capitol; whiskey flowed freely, and many legislative plans were made over steaming bowls of "hot Scotch." Not infrequently men remained all night drinking at the bar. In 1866–1868 both houses of the state legislature were Republican, and I proposed to the committee which had charge of the redistricting of the state the addition of one county to our assembly district. One Democrat rebelled. He threatened to bolt the meeting if politics was to be given consideration in rearranging the districts, but his defiance cooled somewhat when I recalled that in 1856, when he was chairman of the same committee, he had declared that he would gerrymander the state to prevent the Republicans from electing a member. Thereupon I proposed that the committee take a recess for fifteen minutes, during which we visit Young's saloon, then the largest in the capital. Every member of the committee was on his feet on the instant and I ordered "hot Scotch" for the crowd. On the way back one Senator locked arms with me and said I could have any change in the district I desired. (I had not taken any alcoholic liquor until 1852. In 1873, on April 4, I came to the conclusion that it was not good for me and have not touched it since, avoiding even cider.)

On another occasion, in 1868, Horace Greeley came to Madison to deliver an address and was quartered in the same hotel at which a number of the members of the legislature, including myself, were stopping. Late in the evening a party of legislators, whose frequent visits to the bar had brought them to the pitch of noisy hilarity, crowded into my rooms which adjoined Greeley's. At my suggestion the Governor, who had misgivings about the propriety of his appearance in such a gathering, slipped out but was pursued by several members of the party who clattered down the stairs after him. He succeeded in escaping, however, and the pursuers returned to participate in the drinking which followed. I cautioned my colleagues to be quiet, as there was only a door between the room and Greeley's; but the admonition only aroused the retort, "To hell with Greeley!" or loud declarations that "Greeley's all right!" The famous editor observed afterwards that he had been in the worst places in New York City, but none so bad as Madison appeared to be.

My desire to avoid a political career and give my attention to my own affairs appeared to exert an adverse influence, for the more persistently I refused the more I was urged. For several years friends in various parts of the district tried to prevail upon me to enter the field of national politics and to come forward as a candidate for the House of Representatives; but I succeeded, for a time at least, in avoiding that responsibility. Philetus Sawyer, of Oshkosh, who was elected in 1864, had served for ten years. When the state was redistricted Dr. McDill, of Plover, Waupaca County, served for a term, at the conclusion of which he was defeated by Judge Cate, a Democrat of Stevens Point, by a half-dozen votes. Had it not been for the death of my father at this time I am convinced that I could have turned the scale in favor of McDill. When Cate's term expired I was again urged to accept the nomination; but I again refused and Thaddeus Pound, of Chippewa Falls, served for three terms.

At the end of this time Senator Sawyer and Judge Timothy O. Howe, who had been Postmaster-General in 1882, under President Arthur, importuned me to become a candidate for the Republican nomination for Repre-

sentative from the district, a rather desperate chance, in
view of the fact that Pound had made a good record and was
popular among the voters. Some of the local Republican
leaders, among them Thomas Scott of Merrill, and Myron
H. McChord of Shawano, joined in the plea and still others
communicated with me or came to see me. At length, in
the face of my refusals, those who were urging me to become
a candidate took time by the forelock and spread the report
that I would enter the contest. With some misgivings I
finally consented and the announcement was made through
the Milwaukee *Sentinel* that I was in the field.

The uncertainty of politics was very soon brought
home to me. Both Scott and McChord and other Republican leaders in the Wisconsin River valley, who had so
persistently urged me to run, brought out promptly on the
following day Charles M. Webb, later Judge Webb, who was
obviously to receive the support of the organization. The
next day E. L. Brown of Waupaca, announced his candidacy. There were, therefore, four Republicans out for
the nomination: Pound, Webb, Brown, and myself.

The complications that followed in this four-cornered
fight were perplexing. In the first place it was a bad year
for the Republican party generally, the split between
Blaine and Conkling having resulted in the formation of
two factions. In my own case were the internal difficulties. It was quite obvious that the politicians despaired
of beating Pound with any candidate from among their own
number and counted upon my strength with the voters to
weaken his position. The Pound men were quite as convinced that the discord in the Republican ranks would give
them the upper hand. According to the plans that had
been laid, my candidacy was merely to serve this secondary
purpose; and the next strategic move of the Republican

politicians was to put forward Webb in the hope that in the maneuvering between Pound and myself and, possibly, Brown, he would, in racing parlance, take the rail. The odds against me, therefore, seemed to be overwhelming, but I was not ready to give up the struggle.

It was said at the time that the people of Portage County were for E. L. Brown, the convention for Webb, but the delegates for me. When the convention met, Brown, convinced that he could not win, said that his delegates would switch to me after the first ballot, but I told him there would be no second ballot. This proved to be the case. I mustered the necessary majority on the first roll-call.

This upset the plans of the politicians and when I asked the leaders to bring out the vote they assumed an attitude of indifference; said that they did not know whether they would go to the polls or not, and that they might vote the Prohibition ticket. The burden of the entire campaign fell upon me. Pound's friends showed their disappointment by refusing to work at all, and some of the Webb men refused not only to work but to vote. On the other hand, Judge Parks, of Stevens Point, the Democratic candidate, had a very large following and being judge of the district was supported very generally by the lawyers, regardless of politics, who hoped to obtain favors at his hands. In spite of the odds against me I was elected by a majority of two hundred and fifty-six out of a total of forty-seven thousand votes.

In the Wisconsin delegation to the Forty-eighth Congress were three Republicans and six Democrats. The House of Representatives was also controlled by the Democrats by a majority of eighty-one votes and being in the minority we could accomplish little.

In 1884 I was a candidate for a second time. The situation was then much different. The opposition to me had crumbled and after an easy campaign I was re-elected by a majority of four thousand. The fight centered mainly upon the state legislature, control of which the Republicans sought in order that they might designate one of their own number as the successor to Angus Cameron, whose latter term expired in March, 1885. John C. Spooner was the candidate and all the energies of the party were directed toward his election. At this time I began to appreciate the pecuniary demands of politics. The clamor of the political leaders for funds wherewith to carry on the conflict was incessant. Although my own campaign presented few difficulties and my own election was a foregone conclusion, I contributed, to carry on the struggle for control of the state legislature in the interest of Spooner, twenty-two thousand dollars. Our efforts were successful and Spooner assumed office on March 4, 1885.

Much the same situation prevailed in 1886, when Senator Sawyer was up for re-election. My own campaign gave me little concern. I was elected for the third time with a majority of five thousand and might have had a much larger vote if I had not neglected my own affairs to devote my time to the fight for the control of the legislature in the interest of Sawyer. In this we were again successful and Sawyer was returned.

This ended my career in the House of Representatives. It had been sufficiently long to convince me that it was better for me to remain at home and attend to the business affairs which had suffered much by my absence, as my partners were not practical lumbermen and could not altogether fill my place. At the expiration of the third term I announced, in 1889, that I would not accept the nomination again. It probably would have been given me by a unanimous vote, for my political strength appeared to increase with time and the opposition waned in inverse ratio as my majority had gone up. But I had performed such duty as could have been expected of me and had had sufficient experience in public office to know that the sacrifices it involved were to one in my position out of all proportion to the advantages it conferred or the good it enabled one to accomplish. Upon my withdrawal the Republicans nominated Myron H. McChord, who served but one term.

Politics did not cease to interest me altogether, nor did many of the Republicans regard me as having entered into permanent retirement. Once or twice I was urged to become a candidate for gubernatorial honors, but the sacrifice of taking over the responsibilities of another office for two years, although nearer at home, was as great as that involved in going to Washington, and I refused to consider the proposals. I did, however, go to the Republican national convention of 1892, at which Harrison was nominated for the second time, and was also a delegate at large and chairman of the state delegation in 1900, when McKinley was nominated the second time. My first experience of this kind had been gained in 1880, when I was a delegate to the convention which nominated Garfield.

In 1896, after the election of President McKinley, the plan was conceived by the friends of Henry C. Payne, who had been the active force in organizing and directing the Republican campaign, of suggesting to the President his appointment as Postmaster-General. At this time I held no office, but as I had known the President when we were both serving in the House of Representatives I went to Canton in December with Senator Sawyer to see him and to urge Payne's appointment. The President-elect received me cordially and after we had discussed at some length the forthcoming inauguration and experiences in the House, where he had also known my brother, S. M. Stephenson, intimately, I broached the subject of Payne's appointment. He gave us such assurances that both Senator Sawyer and I went away with the conviction that Payne would be chosen for the place. This, however, did not come to pass.

Later on in Washington I called at the White House and ventured to tell President McKinley that he had made a mistake. He said that he had found it to be impossible to carry out his intention and volunteered to appoint Payne to any post in the diplomatic service except London, Paris, or Berlin, which had already been filled. Afterward Payne, at my suggestion, went to the White House and the President repeated the offer to him, but he declined it, preferring to remain in the United States. He finally received his reward, however, at the hands of President Roosevelt, who appointed him Postmaster-General upon the resignation of Charles Emory Smith.

For a number of years, except for incidents such as this, I enjoyed a much needed respite from the cares of public office and was very glad to be left undisturbed in the management of my own business affairs. But in 1898 and 1899, clouds again began to gather upon the political horizon. Senator Sawyer, whom I had known very well not only in Wisconsin but in Washington, and other Republican leaders in the state proposed that I become a candidate for the United States Senate to succeed John L. Mitchell, whose term was to expire in 1899. Sawyer, Payne, Spooner, and various other men for a period of two years had discussed the subject of my possible candidacy. Payne himself wanted the office, but his health was im-

paired and opposition to him from certain classes of people in
the state was so pronounced that the chances of his election
were doubtful. To the plan of putting me forward I was
one of the last to give my approval, and personal considerations would have led me to remain where I was after having
experienced the disadvantages that a congressional career
entailed. But at the solicitation of those whom I regarded
as my friends, and with the purpose of doing what seemed
best from a party point of view, I finally consented to run.

The moral of that undertaking was a valuable one to
me. I discovered for the second time that political assurances were not to be taken at their face value and that I
could not rely upon the promises of my friends — or at
least some of those whom I had regarded as my friends,—
with half as much certainty as I could expect the opposition
of my enemies, confirming and accentuating the conclusions
I had reached as the result of my first campaign for Congress. No sooner had the decision been reached when
the organization leaders switched their support to Quarles
and left me dangling in midair. Perhaps my defeat was
due in some measure to the fact that, unaware of the turn
of events, I had gone to California, where my daughter
christened the battleship "Wisconsin," and so lost valuable
time in the campaign. In any event, Quarles was elected.

To be quite frank, however, I was disappointed, if wiser,
at the end. I felt that I had done much for the Republican
party in the State of Wisconsin from 1858 up to that time,
only to receive scant reward, if one might be permitted to
consider the situation in that lesser light. In itself this
meant little to me, and I had not worked with the expecta-
tion of receiving anything in return, but simply as one
interested in party success. Nor was I indifferent to the
distinction that election to the United States Senate or

service in that body confers. It is an honor worthily sought, the one office in all my political career I would willingly have accepted.

But there was another phase to the situation. It was quite natural, considered in a purely personal light, that I should have felt some resentment against those who had urged me to become a candidate in the interest of the party and then given their support to another,— these, too, the men whom I had assisted in good faith and for whom I had made great sacrifices. Had my defeat been due to popular choice there would have been no occasion for complaint and I should have accepted my fate without murmuring. But it was not a question of popular choice at all. I began to realize for the first time the power and devious ways of the "machine."

CHAPTER XVI

*Experiences in Congress — Friendship with Democratic leaders —
A conference with President Arthur — Congressional economy
— The Navy — Interest in river and harbor improvement —
Possibilities of waterway development — Disappearance of busi-
ness men from public life.*

OF my early experiences in Congress there is little
to relate. The record of what was done during
the six years I served as a member of the House
of Representatives has been set down in detail elsewhere
and it would be superfluous for me to comment upon it
here. The part I played in the legislative deliberations
of this time was a very small one. As a member of the
minority I could accomplish little and moved with the
other Republicans a shadow across the screen, while the
Democratic majority directed the policy of government.

Although I was an uncompromising Republican, and
have been ever since the organization of the party, —
even before, I might say almost with accuracy, when the
Whigs were battling for existence,— I did not feel that
it was incumbent upon me to assert my allegiance to the
extent of arousing the hostility of the Democrats. As a
matter of fact I numbered among them some of my best
friends. This was due partly to my own efforts and partly
to the acquaintanceships I had formed before I thought of
embarking upon a political career. William B. Ogden,
Samuel J. Tilden, William H. Barnum, and many other
prominent members of the party I had known intimately

or had been associated with in a business way. Through them, not infrequently, I learned the political secrets of the Democratic party, subcurrents of thought and purpose not disclosed to the lesser leaders and the rank and file, so that, as a member of the minority, I came to the House under very good auspices. I had the ear of Randall, Tilden's ablest lieutenant; Blanchard, chairman of the river and harbor committee; and others who then directed the destinies of the majority. Many of the Democratic members themselves paid me the compliment of soliciting my aid in passing measures in which they were interested or in ascertaining what plan of action their own leaders had under contemplation. The same was true, in large measure, of the Republican leaders, whom I came to know through men outside of Congress who took no active part in political affairs.

My rather intimate association with Speaker Reed, Tom Reed, as he was better known, then the minority leader and a person of much more impressive personality than William McKinley, I enjoyed more than any other experience during my term of service in the House. Nearly every day we took luncheon together, sometimes by ourselves, sometimes with others. Among the latter was Representative Abram Stevens Hewitt,— "Abe" Hewitt, the great iron master of the firm of Cooper and Hewitt, an ardent Free Trader, who as Reed said, never opened his mouth unless it were "full of raw material." Reed's drollery was a source of constant amusement and, although he was a man of few words, his brief remarks, delivered with a characteristic New England drawl, invariably brought to earth many ambitious legislators who essayed long and lofty flights of oratory. In the six years I served in the House I took luncheon alone but once. If it were not Reed it was some one else I had as my guest, a pleasure which had its benefits as it enabled me to meet and oftentimes to count as friends many of my associates whom I would otherwise have scarcely known.

One of the members of the House at this time was John Arnot, of Elmira, whose father had played a conspicuous part in the construction of the Erie Railroad and whose sister had, late in life, married William B. Ogden. With Arnot, a Democrat, Jesse Spalding, with whom I had been associated in various enterprises, and a general from Pennsylvania, whose name I do not recall, I called on President Arthur late one evening, a visit which I remember with unusual distinctness because of the impression that Arthur made. From eleven o'clock until half-past two in the morning we sat near the entrance of the White House conservatory, talking about various things simply for the pleasure it gave us. President Arthur was an ideal host, suave of manner and possessing a well-developed sense of humor, and enjoyed the conversation as much as ourselves. At midnight we arose to go, but he insisted upon our remaining, telling us of his efforts to renovate the White House and of the discovery in the attic of a table purchased in Andrew Jackson's time. The general from Pennsylvania, who regaled himself with rye whiskey, protesting all the time that bourbon was the proper Democratic drink, achieved so great an admiration for the President before we departed that he declared he would vote for him if the Republicans had the wisdom to nominate him.

There were, of course, many other prominent men in Congress at this time whom it was my good fortune to know, but there is nothing for me to add to what others have said of them.

During these days we had not yet arrived at the point of federal extravagance that has since been attained. The Democrats were ultra-conservative in the matter of spending money and avoided what we have since come to regard as necessary and economical outlay. There was no post-office building at Augusta, the capital of Maine, for example. The city of Oshkosh, Wisconsin, had no federal building and the post-office at Milwaukee was a shambly, inadequate structure which occupied the site on which the Wells Building was subsequently erected. We set out to secure an appropriation for a building there, but met with much opposition and did not carry the struggle to a successful conclusion until the last moment of my three terms of service.

The Navy was also the object of little solicitude on the part of Congress. Representative "Sam" Randall, the Democratic leader in the House, in discussing the administration's naval policy, said that there was no enemy in sight and that, therefore, no Navy was needed. Such was the general point of view, particularly of the Democrats. The fallacy of this course of reasoning was disclosed soon afterward by the outbreak of the Spanish-American War, since which time the policy has been changed. The lesson of that experience, however, has been very largely forgotten. The habitual weakness of the American people is to assume that they have made themselves great, whereas their greatness has been in large measure thrust upon them by a bountiful providence which has given them forests, mines, fertile soil, and a variety of climate to enable them to sustain themselves in plenty, and an isolated position away from the maelstrom of international politics.

It might be well to look with much less complacency upon our own accomplishments and to distrust our own sense of security.

By reason of my early experiences on the lakes, as a sailor, officer, and vessel owner, the part I played in the improvement of harbors, the development of transportation facilities by the use of barges, and the construction of the Sturgeon Bay Canal, I took a very keen interest in the work of the Rivers and Harbors Committee, of which I was a member, and bent my efforts toward securing larger appropriations and making systematic expenditures for waterways. In the forties, as I have said, the Democrats had suspended all federal aid in the improvement of conditions on the lakes, which led every sailor to give allegiance to the Whig party. Since that time Congress had doled out money for this purpose in niggardly fashion.

In 1888, during my service on the House committee, we reported a bill carrying appropriations of twenty-two and one-half millions, six millions larger than any bill framed up to that time. The magnitude of the measure from the point of view then prevailing aroused opposition, and we realized that we had a fight before us to pass it. It fell to me to act in the capacity of whip, to secure pairs between the members opposed to and the members in favor of the bill, and to keep our forces at their places when needed. After working for three days and a half under the five-minute rule, we completed the consideration of only eleven pages. The speaker, pressed for time, was unwilling to proceed further with the debate on the measure and we at length decided to attempt to pass it under a suspension of the rules.

This was difficult of accomplishment. Representative McKinley, for example, afterward President of the United States, said that he was in favor of internal improvements of this character, but that he would not vote for the bill on its final passage under a suspension of the rules. He had no rivers or harbors in his district, he said, and would never be able to explain to all the old women and children why he voted for so large an outlay of money without even considering it. Rather than lose the bill entirely, however, he promised to support it if necessity arose.

On Monday, suspension day, we made our motion and were beaten by nineteen votes. McKinley's name was called, but he did not respond. Among those who opposed the bill was General Brown, from the Wabash district in Indiana, a very able man. He was a member of the Judiciary Committee and had some time before been defeated for the governorship by Hendricks. General Culberson, of Texas, the father of Senator Culberson and chairman of the Judiciary Committee, came to me as we were about to vote and said that he had to go to the White House to discuss an appointment with President Cleveland. We could not sacrifice any votes, and as I was looking about to see whom I could pair with Culberson, General Brown came up.

"Will you pair with General Culberson?" I asked.

"Where is the other man?" he replied. "This motion requires a two-thirds majority and it will take two to pair against me."

For the moment I did not know where to turn, as he was right and there was no other man available for the pair. I therefore took the dilemma by the horns. "Has it come to this," I said, "that the chairman of the Judiciary Committee of the House is not equal to a fellow from an inland district down in Indiana?"

General Brown hesitated a moment, then laughed and said: "All right; I'll go down-town." The vote was saved.

On the second attempt we succeeded in suspending the
rules. McKinley again refused to vote, but we had twenty
more than the necessary two-thirds majority, and the bill
was passed. Our success aroused a deluge of criticism
on the ground of extravagance from all parts of the country.
Nevertheless the appropriations for rivers and harbors
have gone on increasing, reaching in the Fifty-ninth Congress
the enormous total of eighty-three million dollars.

With indiscriminate denunciation of appropriations for
rivers and harbors as "pork-barrel" measures, I have little
patience. Of course there is no gainsaying that every precaution should be taken to avoid useless expenditure, but
the opposition of inland districts which are without navigable rivers or harbors is as short-sighted as the efforts of
other districts to secure as large an appropriation as possible without regard to the value of the improvement contemplated. Wisely designed projects are not for the
exclusive benefit of the limited area in their vicinity. The
Great Lakes, as I had ample occasion to know, were the broad
thoroughfare over which the products of the Middle Western
states, especially before the advent of the railroads, found
their way to the seaboard. It was to the advantage of
Iowa, Illinois, and other inland states as well as to the
states of Wisconsin and Michigan that harbors were
built and shipping facilities extended.

This line of reasoning might well be carried to greater
lengths. The construction of canals and the improvement of navigable rivers will not only obviate some of the
problems which now confront us,— the shortage of cars
and the difficulty of moving crops,— but in the years to
come will cheapen transportation and give comparatively
inaccessible regions an outlet other than the railroads.
To verge upon prophecy, I believe that, as the general

development of the country permits, the great lakes should be connected with the Mississippi River by a ship canal with a system of locks by which the waters of Lake Michigan may be conserved and the level maintained. The Mississippi should provide an adequate waterway from St. Paul to the Gulf of Mexico over which the products of the North and Middle West might be carried directly to foreign markets. To impound the waters of the Great Lakes, the level of which must be maintained, a dam might be built at the head of Niagara Falls, raising the level of Lake Erie; the channel might be narrowed at the outlet of Lake Huron, reducing the waste there; the flow might be checked to some extent in the Straits of Mackinac at the narrowest point near St. Ignace, and precautions taken to retard the flow at the "Soo," the outlet of Lake Superior. Such projects are far in the future, perhaps, but they are worthy of attention. Millions, even hundreds of millions, might be expended annually upon rivers, harbors, and canals in the United States to advantage. At the same time water power, for which there are many sites in northern Wisconsin and the northern peninsula of Michigan, will be developed extensively for the production of electricity, which will take the place of coal and the rapidly dwindling supply of wood.

In 1882, when I first became a candidate for Congress, I went to Ashland near the head of Mucquanicum Bay, where there were three or four sawmills. The water was shoal, not more than twelve feet deep, and Washburn, a village four miles to the north, competed with Ashland for traffic. For fear of disclosing their own lack of harbor facilities the people of Ashland not only made no effort to secure an appropriation, but frowned upon a movement to that end. To accomplish anything it was necessary for

me to take the initiative and I accordingly induced Colonel
Barlow, the engineer in charge of the district with headquarters at Milwaukee, to make a survey for a breakwater designed to prevent the sand from drifting into the
harbor, and for deepening the channel by dredging. Recom-
mendations were made to this effect, the survey was made,
and in 1883 or shortly after I secured an appropriation
to begin the work.

Such was the attitude adopted by many people of the
country toward river and harbor improvement. One of
the most zealous advocates of it was my brother, S. M.
Stephenson, who during his four terms in Congress devoted
much time and effort to the work. It was due largely
to his energy and persistency that a continuing appropriation was made for the maintenance and improvement of
the "Soo" Canal and that many projects on the lakes were
undertaken.

Time has wrought marked changes in the makeup of
Congress since my first years of service in the House of
Representatives. Not only have the men who dominated
the activities of the legislative branch of the government
gone, but there are few of the same stamp to take their
places. Men of experience in the business world — commerce, finance, manufacturing — have given way in great
measure to lawyers, and the effort to eradicate the evils of
the old régime has resulted in a mass of theoretical and
experimental legislation enacted without regard to its effect
upon the productive resources of the country. In my own
time at least eleven of the sixteen members of the Committee on Commerce of the Senate were lawyers, and
only one other than myself had ever had anything to do
with a ship. To one member I suggested that the only
knowledge he had acquired of shipping was confined to a

prairie schooner, and the figure of speech could doubtless have been applied to many others. Small wonder, then, that the statute books have grown bulky with a mass of hastily enacted legislation impossible of enforcement and that men at the head of business institutions look with anxiety to the future.

CHAPTER XVII

*Organization of the Half-breed faction in Wisconsin and election
of La Follette as Governor — Railroad domination of politics —
Financing the La Follette campaign — Nomination and election
of La Follette — Establishment of the* Free Press *as the Half-
breed organ — Eastern corporations enter Wisconsin fight —
La Follette's proposal that I run for the Senate — Half-breed
emissaries — Early reforms accomplished by legislature.*

I NOW come to the latter-day phase of Wisconsin politics: the organization of the Half-breed faction within the Republican party and the election of Robert
M. La Follette as Governor.

The philosophy of the movement which had its beginning in this enterprise has been dealt with by many
exponents and interpreted in many lights. Its evolution
from governmental reform to political dogma has provoked a variety of opinion, stirred commentators to a
fever of activity, and led to prophecies of hope and despair.
Of that controversy I shall have nothing to say. My only
purpose here is to set down the part I played in the undertaking; and in so doing I shall confine myself to a plain
statement of facts, leaving those who may read to draw
their own conclusions.

Internal conditions in the Republican party in Wisconsin in 1898 and 1899 were far from a state of repose.
There was obvious and growing dissatisfaction with the
trend of its affairs. The railroads, public service corporations, and allied interests had come to exert a dominant
influence over the legislative activities of both parties;

and power had become so concentrated in the hands of a
few leaders in the Republican party that they presumed
to direct its destinies to suit their own purposes whether
they ran counter to the desires of the rank and file of the
electorate or not.

In 1866 and 1868, when I was a member of the Assembly, the railroads, then basking in the light of public
favor and looked upon as the harbingers of great prosperity
and industrial development, were, through their agents,
much in evidence at Madison. Their lobbyists had headquarters at the Vilas House, the most important hotel,
and the effects of their activities upon the work of the
legislature were obvious. By the distribution of passes
and granting of favors here and there throughout the
state, this system had been maintained for nearly forty
years; and in time the railroads became so thoroughly
entrenched that they regarded their position as impregnable.

During this constructive period I had been closely
associated with railroad men. Many of them I counted
as my friends. But I thought at the outset and still think
that if their influence had been curtailed it would have
been better for themselves and better for the business of
the state generally. The increase in traffic that would
have followed the adoption of a more liberal policy would
have more than compensated for any immediate losses
they might have sustained; economies would have been
achieved and popular confidence would have supplanted
the distrust in which they came to be held. Nevertheless
they did not elect to follow this course. Instead they
throttled legislation which they considered, in this narrow
light, inimical to them and dominated the legislature. The
boast was made by one of their chief lobbyists that no

bill had passed for sixteen years without their approval; and I believe he was right in this assertion.

But the halcyon days of railroad control were coming to an end. They were no longer the object of popular solicitude and encouragement during the closing days of the last century, and the demand that they pay their just proportion of taxation and submit to the control exercised over all other commercial and industrial institutions grew apace. Like many others I arrived at the conclusion that it would be well for the state to shake off their domination and the incubus of the "inner ring" of politicians which enabled it to maintain itself and for the legislature to exercise greater liberty of action to the end that there might be systematic regulation, not only of the railroads but of public service corporations generally.

To accomplish this, however, required the entire upsetting of the old alignment, a general political upheaval which would restore the power of initiative to the voters. This was no small problem. After weighing it carefully, however, in my own mind and taking measure of the difficulties that would be encountered, I decided on the course I would follow, keeping my own counsel and not consulting, for a time, anyone.

The result was the establishment of the so-called Halfbreed faction as opposed to the Stalwart or regular faction in the Republican party. For several years Albert R. Hall, of Knapp, Dunn County, a Republican who had served in the legislature for several terms, with several others, had been making a futile fight against the influence of the railroads and the coterie which supported them. Robert M. La Follette joined their number, backed Nils P. Haugen for the governorship, and became a candidate for that office twice himself in opposition to the machine. These

efforts to break the ring within which the power of the
dominating corporations was centered were fruitless and
little or no progress was made.

On December 12, 1899, I sent my secretary, Lewis S.
Patrick, to Madison with instructions to see La Follette
and to say to him that it was my suggestion that he again
enter the field for the governorship the following year,
1900. His reply to Patrick was that his health was im-
paired, that he had no money to defray the expenses of
a campaign and that the time was not propitious, that it
was ten years too soon for a concerted effort.

In January, 1900, and again in February, I commissioned Henry Overbeck, Jr., a member of the legislature
from Sturgeon Bay, to go to La Follette and convey to
him a similar message. On both visits he again said it
was too soon, at least five years. Despite his apparent
reluctance to make the attempt in the face of what had
so far proved to be an impregnable opposition, I sent
Overbeck to see him a third time in March with the same
result.

I then enlisted the aid of De Wayne Stebbins, a member of the State Senate from Algoma, in my own district,
who arranged a meeting with La Follette in Chicago during
the latter part of April at the Sherman House. This,
by the way, seemed to be La Follette's favorite method of
avoiding publicity, the risk of which, in most instances,
appeared to me to be so remote as to be scarcely discernible at all. Many of the political plans carried out in
Wisconsin at this time were laid at conferences in Chicago
hotel rooms, the conferees slipping in and out of the city
singly and with the greatest possible secrecy as if the
attention of the world were riveted on their movements,
whereas the world, as a matter of fact, was quite indif-

ferent to them. The meetings might have been held more conveniently at Madison and, so far as I could see, would probably have attracted as little notice.

La Follette was at the appointed place with Edward I. Kidd, the state bank examiner. Before Stebbins could complete what I had instructed him to say La Follette interrupted again, making the objection that the time was not ripe for his candidacy and that he was without funds to make the fight. Stebbins persisted, asking to be heard through before any objections were made and outlined the plan which I had devised. According to this La Follette was to announce his candidacy for the governorship. Stebbins was also to enter the field, but was to withdraw at the proper time after canvassing the northern part of the state. I knew that Henry C. Payne, the leader of the reactionary wing of the Republican party, would bring out a candidate but I was reasonably sure that, with the campaign I proposed, we could defeat him.

When Stebbins had mapped out the plan he handed La Follette $2,500 in currency which I had given him for that purpose. The reluctance which he had exhibited at previous meetings with Patrick and Overbeck vanished. Apparently overcome at the prospect, according to the detailed report of the conference made to me, and with tears running down his cheeks, he declared with confidence that he would be the next governor of Wisconsin.

How well the plan worked out is a matter of political record. Stebbins went on with his canvass in the northern part of the state, to carry on which I gave him $2,500. La Follette confined his efforts to the other parts, as had been agreed upon. To defray the expenses of his campaign I gave $2,500 more, six weeks after the Chicago meeting. These contributions appeared to have fixed a standard. Thereafter when an outlay was needed to meet the difficulties with which the Half-breeds were confronted from time to time, requests were, in most cases, for this precise amount.

These maneuvers mystified the machine politicians, who were, as yet, unaware of the nature of the opposition. The inner council, which had been accustomed to decide what course the party should follow, seemed to realize that they had lost control, but did not understand how it was brought about. In time the Payne candidate withdrew and the others dropped out, leaving the field entirely to La Follette and Stebbins. When this came to pass Stebbins also quit the race. This much having been accomplished, he came to me and offered to return half the money I had given him, the unexpended balance of the contribution I had made to enable him to carry on his campaign. The remainder had been used to defray his traveling expenses. In this, as in all other things, I found him to be a man of absolute integrity.

When the time for the state convention, which was held in Milwaukee, arrived, the Stalwarts had capitulated entirely and La Follette was nominated by a unanimous vote. As his campaign manager and chairman of the state central committee he chose General Bryant, whom he regarded, he said, as a godfather — an idealistic relationship the value of which I was to realize later when, seeking counsel and aid, he clothed me with the attributes of fatherhood.

As a respite for La Follette, whose health was far from good at the time, from the strain of the preconvention campaign, I took about twenty persons, including him and Mrs. La Follette, for an extended excursion on my yacht. Starting at Marinette we went to the "Soo,"

Georgian Bay, and other points on the upper lakes and were away for seven days. The campaign proper, the expenses of which I bore in large part, followed. La Follette was elected and with him a majority of the legislature favorable to our plans.

Having acquired control of the administration, the next problem was to retain it. This required continuous struggle and unfaltering vigilance. The chief handicap of the Half-breed faction was the lack of an organ, an important newspaper which might be used as the medium for conveying to the public its principles and its purposes and by which it might defend itself against attacks, particularly those of the Milwaukee *Sentinel*, the oldest and most influential journal in the state at the time, which was decidedly hostile to the administration. In 1901 the suggestion was made to me that I purchase a controlling interest in the *Sentinel*, which could be obtained for $164,000. I offered to subscribe $50,000 to that end if the remaining $114,000 could be raised by the Half-breed supporters. This could not be done within the two weeks the option was in force and the control of the paper was finally purchased by Charles F. Pfister, one of the stockholders, who continued the policy hostile to the Half-breeds.

La Follette and his friends then set about to establish another newspaper. They obtained a lengthy list of subscribers, most of whom, it came to pass, never paid their subscriptions. Among others, Charles F. Ilsley, whom I had known for fifty years and in whom I had great confidence, agreed to take some stock; and it was pointed out to me that if I would contribute the requisite amount, about $37,000, the paper could be started.

These were no matter-of-fact negotiations. They were carried on in the stress and storm of political conflict and

were illumined with roseate prospects of victory in a praise-
worthy undertaking, the "great cause" which was to live
long after my demise. I was commended for my open-
handed generosity and worthy public spirit in promoting
clean, just government in the commonwealth (the words
are not mine), and pictured as one who had wronged no
man but had suffered much criticism aimed to drive me
out of politics.

At last I went into the publishing enterprise and the
newspaper, called the *Free Press*, was established June
18, 1901. Mr. Ilsley, Mr. Upham, and a few others paid
their subscriptions, but the greater number of the prospective stockholders withdrew, leaving me to bear the
burden alone. I was not an officer in the company, but
took notes for the indebtedness and, having had no experience in the conduct of a newspaper, I soon discovered
that the undertaking was a costly one. The paper "that
was hungered for by a great constituency" and was to
plead the great cause "not of the citizen against the corporation, but of the citizen and the corporation each to
stand equal before the law and each to bear a just burden
of taxation," seemed to meet with the vicissitudes of a
fickle appetite. The $37,000 I contributed to its main-
tenance the first year was increased by $87,000 the second
year and the process continued with disconcerting persistency.

None the less the Half-breeds had their organ and in
that we achieved the primary purpose of the establishment of the *Free Press*, which became an institution of
some political consequence.

The attacks upon La Follette and our faction of the
Republican party were carried on not only from within
the state but from without. Our experiment and the

success we had achieved had attracted the attention of
corporation interests generally, and they contemplated
with some dismay the spread of the propaganda to other
states. In 1902 they originated a movement which came
to be designated the Eleventh Story or Eleventh Floor,
their offices and headquarters being on the eleventh floor
of a building on the corner of Broadway and Wisconsin
streets in Milwaukee. To carry on this work a number of
eastern corporations, it was generally reported, contributed
large sums of money for the purpose of crushing the movement before it could gain headway. It was said that they
had secured, by a large outlay of funds, control of the edi-
torial policy of more than two hundred small newspapers
throughout the state. These ill-advised efforts were not
only futile, but contributed much, I am convinced, to the
success of the Half-breeds. The more energetically they
attacked, the more determined became popular support
of the movement. Had it not been for the resentment
against the interference of the Eleventh Story and the
activities of foreign corporations in the field of state politics, it is not improbable that the Half-breeds would have
been defeated.

The old-line Republicans in 1902 asked me to become
a candidate for the governorship, hoping through me, no
doubt, to encompass the defeat of La Follette. Up to
this time my attitude still puzzled them. In the conduct
of my business I had met men at the head of large industrial and commercial institutions and railroad officials
and was intimately associated with them for a half-century
or more. Many of them were also friendly to me and remained so throughout this period of political upheaval.
That I should have become apparently antagonistic
toward them in a political way they were unable to

understand. None the less, many were broad-minded enough to give me credit for sincerity of purpose and did not hold it against me that I should have aided the Half-breeds. But whether their offer was made as a piece of political strategy or in good faith, I rejected it and held to my course.

Proposals of the same kind were forthcoming from La Follette, who professed a very lively sense of gratitude for what I had done for him and the cause of "clean, just government." In 1902 I met him in Chicago, as I was in the habit of doing frequently at this time, to discuss our political plans. On this occasion he urged me to run for the United States Senate against Spooner. No particular effort, he said, would be required on my part. If I supplied him with funds to carry on the campaign, he explained, I might go to Europe, and during my absence he would bring about my election. This proposal I rejected out of hand. I replied that I had no business in Europe and no intention of going there, but that I had business at home and would not consider the suggestion at all.

In the meantime the political pot bubbled energetically. The emissaries of La Follette found their way to Marinette, some of them coming to my office stealthily by an indirect way and delivering their messages with an impressive air of secrecy, although they could have walked the streets of the city at high noon without attracting any more attention than they did. Among these was Judge Zimmerman, formerly a law partner of La Follette's, whom I have always regarded as an estimable gentleman, Walter Hauser, and Harvey Clark. Sometimes the emissaries departed with a "package of papers," the accepted designation for one of the $2,500 contributions the advancement of the "great cause" so often seemed to require, leaving the city as stealthily as they had entered it.

About this time also, when La Follette came to Appleton and De Pere on a speech-making tour, I sent Mr. J. A. Van Cleve to the latter place with $1,000 in currency which he gave to La Follette at the conclusion of his address to defray the expenses of his campaigning.

What was accomplished in a legislative way during the first two years of Half-breed control of the state government was well set forth by Governor La Follette himself:

We have not accomplished everything hoped for. We have made great strides toward better government and secured much that is of the highest value. Not in a quarter of a century has a more important piece of legislation been enacted than the law which taxes railroad property in Wisconsin upon the same basis as other taxable property.

We could not secure primary election legislation to be immediately effective, but we have passed a bill which the people will, I trust, adopt in the general election of 1904. Should they do this, it will consummate the most far-reaching and valuable public measure for representative government enacted in Wisconsin since her admission into the Union.

We have passed many laws of special excellence besides, notwithstanding the obstruction encountered in the Senate. They will receive merited attention when the work of this session is reviewed in detail. A large number of bad bills have been beaten and vetoed, the evil in which the public will never fully know.

We have failed in one great piece of legislation, which is not dead, nor does it even sleep for a day. The work goes on and will not halt or stop till the transportation taxes are reduced and equalized in Wisconsin. But even in this we have made phenomenal progress and advanced farther in a few months than any other state, or even the general government, in a decade.

All this history of political accomplishment, I was assured, "would have been a blank page" but for my aid and influence.

So far, so good. These specific reforms were of benefit to the state and were a part of the work we had set out to do. Looking backward, however, I am not now so certain that I would advocate a primary election law as I was then. It is the sort of legislation of which everything good can be said and which arouses popular interest; but experience has proved, I think, that it is not practicable. It increases the burden of political obligation unnecessarily. The people, as a rule, except under the stimulus of an extraordinary contest, will not go to the polls twice to fill the same office. July Fourth, the Christmas holidays, and general elections are the only occasions when they will give their attention to other things than their daily work. The primary vote is always but a small proportion of the total vote in either party. And I am not sure that this method of selecting candidates is the most effective. A convention of selected delegates can proceed with greater deliberation and more sense of responsibility than the people as a whole, who are often times swayed by meretricious influences or guided by sympathy which may or may not properly have place in the selection of public officers. By way of illustration, I might be expected to act with greater caution in selecting a foreman for one of my mills than the workmen themselves and with greater regard for the permanency of the institution. That, however, is a large question which has no place here.

CHAPTER XVIII

Half-breeds successful in 1902 and 1904 — Demoralization of Stalwarts — Rifts in the reform party and early defeats — Setback in Third Congressional district — Fight over election of successor to Senator Quarles — Half-breeds pick La Follette for Senate — His apparent reluctance to leave Wisconsin — Lieutenant-Governor Davidson picked for slaughter — Another Half-breed defeat — Campaign for unexpired term of Senator Spooner — Discord among the reform leaders — My election to Senate.

THE Half-breed faction continued its successes without serious interruption and dominated the Republican party. In 1902 they won without great difficulty, and La Follette was re-elected governor together with a legislature the majority of which was sympathetic with our purposes. The opposition, however, although badly demoralized, did not abandon the conflict. They continued their efforts and preserved an organization sufficient, at least, to take advantage of mistakes growing out of the overconfidence of the Half-breed leaders.

In 1904, when La Follette was nominated at the Madison convention, the old-line Republicans withdrew and established a rump convention which nominated S. A. Cook. This gave rise to the question of regularity which was taken before the Supreme Court. La Follette was declared to be the nominee on the Republican ticket, the rump convention was held to be irregular, and Cook, who was as honorable a man as I ever knew, accepted the decision without a word of protest and withdrew. The

Stalwarts, or regular Republicans, thereupon nominated former Governor Schofield, who received only twelve thousand votes.

In the third congressional district the Half-breeds met with defeat. Their candidate, J. J. Blaine, was pitted against Joseph W. Babcock, against whom the strength of the Half-breed faction was concentrated. W. D. Conner, chairman of the state central committee, wrote to me during the campaign, saying that a delegation from the district had assured him that with a fund of fifteen hundred dollars for expenses they could defeat Babcock and suggested that if I would contribute half the amount he would contribute a similar sum personally, as the committee itself was without funds. I sent my check for one thousand dollars. The efforts of the Half-breed leaders were futile. It was disclosed afterward that Henry Overbeck and thirty-eight game wardens, who were in the employ of the state government, went into the district on a single train to participate in the fight. Nevertheless Babcock was elected. Despite the part I had played in the campaign we remained good friends up to the time of his death. More than once in later years he said that the mistake of his life had been not to have thrown his support to me when the senatorial campaign was on in 1898. It would have prevented many misunderstandings, he explained, and saved him many regrets.

The Stalwarts, who apparently had an unlimited campaign fund, were being aided, according to reports current at the time, by interests outside the state. It was said that they had at their disposal two or three hundred thousand dollars contributed by eastern railroad corporations who were viewing with alarm the interest aroused by the fight in Wisconsin to equalize taxation and compel the

transportation interests to bear their just proportion of
the burden.   In any event, they made a very energetic and
systematic canvass in 1904.   But their efforts were un-
availing.   We won by a majority of 50,000 and it was
estimated, and I think accurately, that we received the
votes of 40,000 independent or "fair-minded" Democrats
who supported La Follette and the ticket generally.   Of
the popular attitude toward the issues we had raised there
could be no question.

The important political problem before the legislature,
which we controlled, was the election of a Senator to succeed
Senator Quarles.   Governor La Follette had always said that
he would not go to Washington.   The question thereupon
arose whether enough strength could be mustered to elect me.

Inexplicable difficulties began to arise.   Governor La
Follette took the attitude that his aid would not be sufficient to bring about my election because of the opposition
of two men, H. L. Ekern and E. N. Warner, the latter the
member from his own assembly district in Madison.   He
expressed keen regret over his inability to induce Warner
to come to my support; and that insurmountable obstacles
should have stood in the way of my going to the Senate,
he said, "almost broke his heart."

While this discussion was going on I pursued a noncommittal course, saying that I would not urge that any
action be taken at that time.   I merely suggested to La
Follette and the other Half-breed leaders that I might
obtain eight or ten Stalwart votes, as many of the Stalwarts
were very friendly to me personally and bore me no ill
will because of my support of the reforms instituted
through the Half-breed faction.   This immediately aroused
vehement protest from the Half-breed leaders, who had
obviously arrived at such a point of confidence in their

ability to dominate the politics of the state that they fore-
swore everything that savored of compromise. For every
Stalwart vote gained, they insisted, ten Half-breed votes
would be lost. It began to be apparent to me that the
Half-breeds had other plans.

The legislature met in January, about which time
Governor La Follette asked me to come to Milwaukee
to meet some of the members and other political leaders.
Lenroot, then speaker of the Assembly, Walter Hauser,
Judge Chynoweth, Mr. Myrick, editor of the *Free Press*,
and several others were at the conference. For three
hours plans for the senatorial election were discussed,
during all of which time I listened but said nothing. The
conclusion was reached that neither I nor anyone else
except La Follette could be elected, and he again insisted
that he did not wish to and would not go to the United
States Senate.

Lenroot and some of the others then proposed that
La Follette be elected and that, in the meantime, they
canvass the legislature to ascertain whether a sufficient
number of votes could be obtained to elect me, in which
event La Follette would decline the office and I would go to
Washington instead. The talk went on up to midnight.
During the entire conference the only observation I made
was that I could secure eight or ten Stalwart votes. Invariably this met with the declaration that it would be a
disadvantage rather than an advantage upon the assump-
tion that the Stalwart votes would alienate the Half-breeds,
a rather extreme supposition, to my mind. As it was I
lacked only two votes short of a majority, but this seemed to
have no weight in the council.

La Follette was elected Senator in January, 1905. So
far as I could observe no effort was made to elect anyone

else. I had learned still another lesson on the uncertainties of politics.

Even after his election La Follette was obviously reluctant to relinquish the governorship and did not go to Washington for a year after he was commissioned to represent the state in the upper house of the national legislature. During this time, the year of 1905, Wisconsin had only one Senator.

The reasons for this reluctance I will not attempt to explain. About this time, however, I began to hear from other quarters. Lieutenant-Governor Davidson, who was associated with Hall at the very outset of the reform movement which led to the creation of the so-called Half-breed faction, told me that some of the La Follette leaders had come to him and said that La Follette would give up the governorship and go to the Senate if he would agree not to become a candidate for the office of Governor again in 1906 after he served for the remainder of La Follette's term,— a proposition which, to my mind, at least, was indefensible from any point of view. Subsequently, I was told, La Follette himself went to Davidson and said that he would resign and go to the Senate if Davidson would give his word that he would not run in 1906. Davidson replied that he would make no such agreement if he never became Governor of the state.

On the evening of the same day Governor La Follette issued a call for an extra session of the legislature to make some slight alterations in a bill. This was done and La Follette immediately afterward resigned the office of Governor and went to Washington. Davidson succeeded him as Governor, taking office on January 1, 1906.

Then came the aftermath of this particular episode. When time for the canvass of 1906 arrived, Davidson declared his candidacy and La Follette decided to fight. He held a conference in Chicago with Haugen, Myrick, editor of the *Free Press*, Lenroot, and one or two others, and subsequently Lenroot was brought out as a candidate for Governor in opposition to Davidson, whose standing in the state and whose early efforts in support of the reform movement availed nothing against the decree of the so-called progressive Republican leaders. He was slated for sacrifice for no apparent reason. La Follette took the stump in behalf of Lenroot and in his speeches bitterly denounced Davidson, declaring that he was not fit for the office.

Having watched this shifting of events from the background, I told La Follette that he had made a serious political blunder in bringing out Lenroot to oppose Davidson and that the people of the state were fair-minded and would support the latter. The *Free Press*, too, espoused Davidson's cause. How far the La Follette plans went awry may be gathered from the results of the primary election. Davidson received 100,583 votes; Lenroot, 61,178. In the election proper Davidson's plurality was 80,000 votes. The record he achieved during his administration bore out, I still believe, the predictions I had made to La Follette. A number of excellent laws for the regulation and taxation of public service corporations and the regulation of freight rates were enacted, some of which have served as a pattern for other states.

Whether or not I entered into the calculations of La Follette when he was wavering between retaining the governorship and going to Washington I will not say, but one or two incidents seemed to indicate that the possibility of my election to the Senate in the event of his refusal to go was as much a consideration as the possibility of

Davidson becoming a candidate for Governor in case he did go. His decision to choose the latter course appeared to me, at least, very sudden; for shortly before his resignation as Governor he assured me that he had no intention of going to the Senate.

In the autumn of 1905, when La Follette was still in this undecided frame of mind, Judge Chynoweth, one of his lieutenants, came to Marinette to see me. The ostensible purpose of his visit was to inspect a large barn my brother, S. M. Stephenson, had erected in Menominee, to obtain ideas for the improvement of a farm he intended to give his son. Chynoweth's farm was not much larger than the barn itself and it was about as reasonable to pattern a log house after a skyscraper as to suppose that he was to gain any practicable information; but these political errands always had to have an object other than the real one. On the first visit he came on Saturday and remained at my daughter's house over Sunday. On the second he remained at my house all night. The conversation covered a wide range of subjects, but the nucleus of it was a statement made by Chynoweth that La Follette was to call the extra session of the legislature, coupled with the assertion that the Governor had no intention of going to the Senate.

"Who will be elected in his place?" I asked Chynoweth.

"I don't know," he replied; "but La Follette still thinks you cannot be elected."

To this I made no response and the discussion veered to other subjects. So the verbal sparring went on for the greater part of Sunday, while he was at my house, during which time at intervals he reverted to the question of the forthcoming extra session and the possibility of La Follette's abandonment of his senatorial plans. My question invariably met with the same reply, but I vouchsafed no comment and offered no suggestions.

At length, unable to elicit an expression of my own intents and purposes, Chynoweth said bluntly: "What have you in mind? I can see that you are thinking of one thing and talking about others."

"Well, Chynoweth," I replied gravely, "Talleyrand says that language was made to conceal thoughts."

That concluded the discussion. La Follette's emissary — I assumed that he was acting in that capacity — went home no wiser concerning my plans than when he came. The extra session of the state legislature was called and La Follette began his senatorial career soon afterward.

John C. Spooner, the senior Senator from Wisconsin, resigned his office on March 4, 1907. When the announcement was made a number of the leading Republicans of Wisconsin telegraphed and wrote to me urging me to become a candidate to succeed him for the unexpired portion of his term. This I decided to do and on March 4 made a public announcement asking for the appointment for the remaining two years. At the same time I wrote to Senator La Follette,— with whom my relations were still friendly,— informing him of my decision to become a candidate. He replied that he had expected me to take that course and assured me that he would do all that he could to assist me. He found it necessary, he said, to go to Pittsburgh to deliver an address, after which he would come to Madison. In the mean time his law partner, Rogers, expressed the opinion that Hatton would be elected.

In any event I was not to have the field to myself. In a day or two four other candidates entered the lists: Representative Cooper, of the First Congressional District; Representative Esch, of the Seventh; Mr. Lenroot, of Superior;

and State Senator Hatton, of Waupaca.   All of us opened headquarters at Madison.

At the outset I had the advantage over the others. About twenty votes had been assured me, one or two more than any of the others could muster. After a time the legislature went into caucus and met night after night without any change in the relative strength of the candidates. In due time Senator La Follette arrived in Madison, called in his friends in the legislature and asked them to vote for me. The La Follette influence, however, appeared to be very ineffective at this time, for it brought about no appreciable change in the situation. To what extent it was exercised others may surmise for themselves. Senator La Follette himself said that he could do no more than he had, because the men generally recognized as his followers or supporters were his friends. A sudden delicacy of feeling, I suppose, forbade any zealous attempt to influence the action or mold the convictions of these men whom the outer world had erroneously regarded as parts of a well organized political machine. That, at least, was the impression I received; and I was given to understand that the idea that La Follette's aid was more than sufficient to turn the scale in my favor was without foundation. Neither did the fact that the voluminous political history of the preceding seven or eight years would have been a "blank page" but for my aid and influence count for anything.

At the end of seven weeks, during which time none of the contestants had made any marked progress, the legislative caucuses having been entirely fruitless, a committee of five was appointed by the two houses to wait upon the candidates at the Avenue Hotel. Since the legislature itself had failed to break the deadlock, Duncan McGregor, as chairman and spokesman of the committee, suggested that the five candidates themselves solve the problem by choosing one of their own number to bear the honors, the other four withdrawing from the contest. If this were not done, he said, the legislature would take matters into its own hands entirely without regard for any of the candidates and set out to elect a Senator in whatever way it deemed best.

When McGregor had concluded his statement the committee withdrew and the five candidates remained in the room. For some time a perfunctory conversation about everything except the subject under consideration was carried on, each one avoiding taking the initiative in proposing a solution of the perplexing problem and each refusing to relinquish any advantage. At length the conversation lapsed and silence fell upon the gathering. Each one sat back and waited for another to make an opening. Mr. Cooper finally broke the spell which seemed to have settled upon us and brought out the ludicrous aspect of the conference by observing that he had been in many political assemblages, but never in one where there was so much loud talking. This provoked a laugh. On the heels of it I ventured the suggestion that I was the oldest of the five candidates and that if I were elected for the unexpired term of Senator Spooner I would not be a candidate in 1908. This would enable the other four to go before the people in the forthcoming primaries on an even basis. The proposal met with the inevitable silence. No one agreed to anything; no one had an opinion to express. As the situation was obviously hopeless, we all withdrew after a time and went to our headquarters.

For two weeks longer the struggle continued. On May 15, the other four candidates and their friends came together in the office of the State Treasurer and agreed that

Hatton was the strongest candidate and threw their support to him. I went my own way. On the same day, when the legislature met, Hatton received fifty votes — two short of the number necessary. This was brought about, it was said at the time, by the withdrawal of two members of the legislature by one of the progressive leaders hostile to Hatton. On the following day, May 16, I received fifty-five votes, three more than a majority. At noon on May 17, I was formally elected.

Under the circumstances I felt that the election was unconditional so far as political promises were involved. I had announced at the outset of the fight that if I were elected for the two years without opposition I would not become a candidate at the regular election, and I reiterated the promise at the fruitless conference of the five candidates at the Avenue Hotel in Madison. The conditions were not observed. I therefore felt quite free to do as I chose in the future and I followed that course.

CHAPTER XIX

Early events in senatorial career — Failure to arrive at working agreement with La Follette over patronage — Requests for aid for La Follette presidential campaign — Convention of 1908 — The La Follette platform — Nomination of Taft — The senatorial campaign of 1908 — Announcement of my candidacy.

A T the outset of my service in the Senate the progress of political events was smooth enough. One of the first men to congratulate me upon my election was Assemblyman Warner who, Senator La Follette had said, was opposed to me in 1905. On the day after the election Senator La Follette himself telegraphed his congratulations and a week or two later he wrote to me in the friendliest possible vein, saying, among other things: "My dear Senator: It is good to write that down and to know that nothing can ever change it. At last after a quarter of a century justice has been done. I wanted to visit with you and talk it all out, but it will keep and we shall go over it together many times."

It began to appear that, despite the misunderstandings that had arisen and the mistakes that had been made, the prospect was clearing and I was willing to look forward rather than backward.

But it was not long before I became aware that the purposes of La Follette and of the La Follette organization were not my purposes. This became apparent when the problems of patronage, the first to arise, came up for solution. For the convenience of both of us I desired

235

to come to some sort of understanding regarding offices.
This could best be accomplished, it seemed to me at the
time, by the exchange of districts, La Follette being more
familiar with conditions in the Western district, which had
been allotted to me, than I was. This or any other definite
arrangement he seemed to be reluctant to make. "I think
it will be a nice thing," he said, "for us both to join in
making appointments, because I have no doubt we can
agree. Of course Spooner and I could not do that."

Of this I was not so certain as he seemed to be. I
objected mainly on the ground that it would be impossible
for me to ascertain what his wishes might be in a particular case when he was away on the Chautauqua circuit,
to which he gave much attention during this period, or
for him to find out what I might desire.

Nevertheless, choosing what I considered to be the
wiser course, I deferred to his judgment in certain instances
when appointments were to be made in my own district,
— with what effect the following two incidents will show.
Not long after my election I was asked by the Post-Office
Department to make a recommendation for the appointment of a postmaster at Highland. I communicated with
Senator La Follette, who suggested that I write to Dwight
Parker, cashier of a bank at Fennimore, Grant County,
and also J. J. Blaine, of Boscobel. Parker named a man
whom I recommended and he was appointed. Senator
La Follette then told me I had made a mistake.

"You told me that Parker was all right," I said. "How
in thunder could I tell!" Thereupon he shifted to Parker
the blame for the error, as he considered it.

About the same time the term of the postmaster at
Boscobel had expired. I wrote to J. J. Blaine, asking
whom the people wanted for the office, a Half-breed having

been mentioned for the place. After about a month Blaine replied that no decision had been reached with respect to the appointment. In response to another letter from me he said that the postmaster then in office was not much of a politician but a good fellow, and that the majority of Republicans in the town would approve of his reappointment, although no mistake would be made if the Half-breed who had been mentioned were recommended. He himself, he said, did not wish to take part in the affair because he was to run for the legislature. He was subsequently elected and what he has done is a matter of public record. After these two episodes I chose to make my own appointments.

Long before this Senator La Follette's political horizon had broadened. The success of the Half-breed faction of the party in Wisconsin, which came to be more mellifluously designated "progressive Republicanism" elsewhere, was complete within that restricted field and he had been industriously sowing the seed of the "great cause" elsewhere in the Middle West from the Chautauqua platform. In 1905 he visited twelve states in the Middle West and reported that "It is encouraging to find how deep an impress our work in Wisconsin has made upon all this section of the country and how ready people seem to take hold for organization. I try every place I go to start organization."

In his travels, he added, he was surprised to find how many people knew the *Free Press* and its work. "It stands out before the country almost alone as the fearless, able, incorruptible advocate of the kind of government Lincoln proclaimed on the field of Gettysburg." The growing deficit was not disconcerting. "It cannot fail," he said. "If such a paper with its high purpose and conspicuous ability cannot succeed as a business enterprise, then God help our poor country."

For my part in this enterprise I was paid a tribute in terms so glowing that I hesitate to repeat them here. "Then there is another side and a better and nobler side to this *Free Press* proposition," he added. "Mr. Stephenson cannot overlook it, and it is going to stand out as one of the greatest and most enduring things in his remarkable life. It is this: the *Free Press* is a part of the history of the reform movement which began in Wisconsin and has become the dominant idea in the great decade upon which we are now entered as a nation. The *Free Press* stands to-day as the only distinct representative of that idea among the newspapers of the country.

"Mr. Stephenson made this paper possible. The paper made the fight for reform in Wisconsin a potential fact in the nation. It is the best supporter of the President who has taken up the issue. Mr. Stephenson has amassed an immense fortune. It is a great thing to have acquired a great fortune honestly in these days. But he is a multi-millionaire by sheer force of his business ability and sagacity.

"Others prominent in the world of finance (whose names I forbear to mention) Senator La Follette went on to say, "have secured their fortunes in violation of plain criminal statutes. Isaac Stephenson will be long remembered for his great business ability. But man cannot live by bread alone. Man's best fame cannot rest on wealth alone. In the last four years he has founded and maintained at great cost a great newspaper which is doing a noble work for the emancipation of government from graft, which is bringing government back to the people, which day by day is saying to the big corporations of Wisconsin: 'Con-

duct your business in obedience to the law and keep your
corrupting hands off legislation.'

"To do this thing and make this paper a moral and
political force in the restoration of government to the citizen
is to wield a greater power and render a greater service
to his state and country than falls to the lot of many men.
The establishing and maintaining of the *Free Press* is Mr.
Stephenson's best monument. It is an act of patriotism.
His family and his friends and the history of his time will
cherish it as the really greatest work of a great life."

The Senate, also, offered La Follette a wider field of
activity. "You say the fight is getting to be a big one
there," he wrote before my election to that body. "It
is big enough here. And when I have to struggle against
all the Stalwarts in the departments, in Congress, the United
States Senate,— an atmosphere that is generally charged
with poison,— you can realize that it is a good hard proposition for a fellow to go up against single-handed and
alone. If you were on the ground here with me, I should
feel very confident; but you know I will keep up the fight
until the clock stops, anyway."

With this larger movement, despite these flattering
allusions, I was not sympathetic. In Wisconsin the old
railroad-corporation crowd, the inner ring which controlled
party affairs to the exclusion of all others, had been fairly
routed and some good laws were placed on the statute
books. There the task ended for me. I did not choose
to purify the politics of other states. Senator La Follette,
however, had larger political aspirations.

During the holiday season of 1907, when I was in
Marinette, A. H. Dahl and H. L. Ekern, two of La Follette's friends, came to see me. The purpose of their visit
was to raise money for a campaign in the interest of Sena-

tor La Follette as a presidential candidate. Both professed to be enthusiastic over the prospects of his success. Ekern counted upon him to carry Wisconsin, Iowa, Minnesota, the Dakotas, New Jersey, most of California,—nearly all the western states. I was of another mind. On January 4, however, I gave them one thousand dollars. At the same time, Dahl asked me to give Lenroot $2,000, saying that he was in need of money to defray the expenses of his campaign. I was under no obligation to Lenroot and did not feel called upon in any way to come to his aid and said so.

The enthusiasm of the La Follette admirers, measured by their requests for financial assistance to carry on his preconvention campaign, was almost boundless. In January, 1908, some of them proposed that I contribute $250,000 to defray the expenses of this political venture. During the same month Ekern came to Washington and asked me to subscribe a very large sum. La Follette's nomination, he thought, would be a foregone conclusion if the money were forthcoming to make the fight. For several hours we discussed the plan at the hotel in Washington at which I was living at the time, and he urged me to supply the necessary funds. As he talked he gradually scaled down the amount sought until it reached twenty-five thousand dollars.

The reduction did not bring his ideas any more into harmony with mine. There was no reason why I should shoulder the burden of attempting to nominate La Follette as the exponent of the progressive cause and I was not disposed to do it. Moreover, I was firmly convinced that the chance of his being nominated under any circumstances, however strong and general the reaction against the old school of politics might have become, was

fund or no fund, extremely remote. The humming of
the presidential bee had been too seductive to his admirers.
How correct I was in this judgment may be gathered from
the fact that he received twenty-five out of the twenty-six
votes cast by the Wisconsin delegation at the national
Republican convention and no more.

The results of these negotiations, which were fruitless,
may or may not have been reflected in the events that
immediately followed. I give them simply as the background of events which more directly concerned me. From
them I draw no conclusions nor make any deductions.

In 1908 I was elected one of the four delegates at large
from Wisconsin to the national convention, a responsibility which I did not seek and would rather have avoided.
It was my intention at this time to hold no more political
offices. I had had more than my share and it was of more
immediate importance to me to remain at home and give
my attention to my business.

Nevertheless I went, and my experiences began to indicate the change in drift of sentiment among the leaders
of the La Follette group. Ekern had written to me in
Washington, saying that he had made a contract with the
Stratford Hotel Company for quarters for the state delegation and asked me to guarantee the payment of $2,700.
This was contrary to the practice I had observed in my
business affairs for more than forty years, during which
time I endorsed but one note and that only for the reason
that the holder did not wish to be paid for a year. I did
not care to make an exception to this rule and so informed
Ekern, but I agreed to pay one thousand dollars toward
defraying the expenses of the delegation. A week or two
later he informed me that he had secured quarters at the
Grand Pacific and I sent the $1,000. I secured accommoda-

tions at the Palmer House, where I had stopped for twenty-eight years while in Chicago.

Curiously enough, as it seemed to me at the time, I was never able to penetrate to the inner recesses of the rooms at the Grand Pacific. It was not generally known at the time, I believe, that La Follette was in Chicago; but I learned later that he and Representative Cooper had been closeted together for two or three days, drafting a platform in which the principles of progressivism from his point of view were embodied. I went to the hotel several times during the progress of the convention, but failed to see either Mr. Cooper or Senator La Follette. Whenever I sought the former I was given evasive replies and told that it would be difficult for me to find the rooms. At the same time the platform committee of the convention brought in its report, which was unanimous, Representative Cooper presented the La Follette platform, which excited little attention, as it was regarded very much as a one-man affair.

The state delegation formally assembled at the Grand Pacific Hotel on Monday, the day before the opening of the convention, and an effort was made to elect me chairman. Refusing the honor, I insisted that some regard be shown for the German element of the state, which had not had its proportion of offices, and proposed that Col. William C. Brumder, of Milwaukee, whom I scarcely knew, be chosen. He said that the distinction belonged to me, but I persuaded him to accept it and made the motion to that end, which was carried.

When the convention met I voted for La Follette, as did three other members of the delegation, under our instructions; fourteen voted for Sheldon, of Nebraska. I doubt whether any of the fourteen knew anything about

Sheldon, but the strategy of the situation apparently demanded this action. How futile these efforts were, if they were in the interest of La Follette, is obvious in the light of what actually happened. Knox had Pennsylvania; Cannon had Illinois and Fairbanks had Indiana; but when the time came for voting, the overwhelming sentiment of the convention had become plainly manifest and everybody went for Taft.

With this choice I was well pleased. As Governor of the Philippines, and as Secretary of War, Mr. Taft had shown his capacity for handling large affairs successfully. The troublesome problem of the Philippines, complicated by the friar lands question, he had solved admirably. He accomplished the novel task of establishing a colonial government in the islands and set thereby an example for the nations of the world. The part he played in the construction of the Panama Canal was no less important. When the undertaking appeared to be on the verge of collapse because of the desertion of the civil engineers and the opposition of the railroads, he brought order out of the chaos by the appointment of Colonel Goethals and making military authority paramount. Since his term as President I see no reason for changing my opinion of him. Unscrupulous opposition within the ranks of his own party and the chaos of general political upturning made achievement all but impossible; and to these conditions, rather than to any lack of capacity on his part, was his defeat due. Under normal conditions, and with a united party behind him, I have no doubt that his record of accomplishment as President would be no less noteworthy than his record as Secretary of War.

With the convention out of the way — to return to my own fortunes, — interest in Wisconsin centered upon the

senatorial situation.   For a long time, as I have said, I had
no intention of entering the field.   Many persons had urged
me to run and I had received communications from various
parts of the state with promises of support if I would become
a candidate.   In March or April, 1908, I had told Senator
La Follette that many of my friends were trying to induce
me to make the race again.   His only response was the
rather curt question: "Are they?"   By this time I had
begun to understand some of the intricacies of politics.

The situation in Wisconsin was somewhat complex.
Senator Hatton had announced his candidacy for the full
term as far back as May 17, 1907, when I was elected to
serve for the unexpired term of Senator Spooner.   S. A.
Cook, of Neenah, another candidate, had been hard at
work canvassing the state for a year or more.   Four days
after the Republican national convention the papers carried the announcement of McGovern's candidacy.   It
was assumed by persons who knew something of the situation that McGovern was the La Follette candidate,
although most of the political leaders were of the opinion
that Hatton was the stronger of the two.   On the surface
it appeared that some of the La Follette people were for
Hatton, but the results of the election belied this supposition.   Hatton carried his own county, Waupaca,
Superior, La Crosse, and the little county of Rusk, four in
all, although he made an aggressive campaign.   Cook,
who was in the good graces of the old soldiers and the
dairymen, visited every town in the state and ran second.

Upon my return from the Chicago convention I stopped
at Milwaukee in response to telephone messages concerning
business matters and while there met McGovern in the
Free Press office.   We talked over the situation and I
made the prediction that he could not win.

Even at this time and for ten days after the convention I had not arrived at the conclusion that I would become a candidate. But I kept my own counsel and said nothing, even to the members of my family. I was free to act as I chose. The candidates for Spooner's seat during the preceding year not having accepted the proposal I had made to withdraw if I were elected without opposition, there was no promise standing in the way of my making another attempt.

The wisdom of such a course, however, was still to be determined. About two weeks after the convention, when I was in Milwaukee again, I met several of my close friends and in the course of a discussion of the political situation said that I had been thinking of announcing my candidacy for the Senate. There were considerations for and against it which I shall not dilate upon here. Some of my friends seemed to lean toward the latter view, but the discussion did not seem to clarify the situation. After a half-hour no conclusion had been reached and I brought the talk to an end by saying, "I am a candidate." A short statement to that effect was given to the press and I went back to Marinette on the evening train.

CHAPTER XX

Difficulties of primary campaign — Hostility of the La Follette organization — Setting up an organization and obstacles encountered — Tactics of opposition — Election and repudiation of primary by La Follette forces — Investigation by state legislature — Standards of propriety in campaign expenditure — Vindication by investigating committee — Investigation by United States Senate — Retirement from politics.

IT was not long before I came to the realization that in my campaign for the Senate I was confronted by many perplexing difficulties. If the odds were against anyone, they were against me. Other candidates had the advantage of having been long in the field and had accomplished much in the way of perfecting an organization and canvassing the state. I, on the contrary, had done nothing, and the men with whom I had been associated and whom I had aided in the past were against me. If the fight was to be made, it was to be made by me alone.

Obviously I could no longer expect the support of the Half-breed faction, which had been absorbed by the La Follette machine. The indifference which the so-called progressive leaders had hitherto displayed crystallized into open opposition. On the other hand, some of my opponents had been in the field for months and had made a definite and systematic plea for the support of some of the classes of voters upon whom I depended for success.

It was necessary for me to start from the very beginning, form an organization of some kind and make up for the time that had been lost to overcome the handicap obtained by those who had been in the field before me. W. D. Connor, who had been chairman of the Republican state central committee for four years, controlled the machinery of the Republican organization and was in possession of the voting lists and names of the leaders in every county. My efforts to secure these and his good will were to no purpose.

The time was short and I set out to build up the machinery of campaigning with the least possible delay. E. A. Edmunds, of Appleton, I placed in charge of the organization work. J. A. Van Cleve, of Marinette, and J. H. Puelicher, of the Marshall and Ilsley Bank of Milwaukee, took charge of the expenditures. We were all more or less at sea in the matter of the details of the work and had to obtain information as best we could without considering the cost.

Letters were written to every postmaster and county clerk with requests for poll lists and the names of voters. Sometimes they were obtained; many times they were not. Wherever possible, men were employed to bring together and take charge of a local organization through which the questions at issue could be put before the electorate. Campaign literature was distributed in more or less haphazard fashion because of the difficulties confronting us, and campaign paraphernalia was sent out in great quantities. In Milwaukee alone I had constantly employed more than a score of clerks and stenographers who did nothing but attend to this work and the correspondence. The expenses for postage exceeded twelve thousand dollars. Probably there was no campaign that had ever been carried on in a more wasteful or extravagant manner considered from a business point of view; but there was no time for checking up, no opportunity to ascertain whether the money were being expended to the best advantage, or, possibly, whether in some cases it were being expended at all. Time was too valuable for us to attempt to retrace our steps or to ascertain in what respect the methods we were employing were defective.

It would have been to my advantage to go into every county in the state, but even this was impossible because of the very pressing business affairs which engaged my attention at this time. For twenty of the sixty days I was out of the state. During the last five days preceding the primary election I was able to visit only seven out of the seventy-one counties. Neither were some of my opponents very scrupulous in the methods they used to fight me. The report was assiduously spread that I was seventy-nine years of age and that I could not remember my own name without serious reflection. It is true that I was seventy-nine years of age. As most men at this time of life have retired from both business and politics, if they have been so fortunate as to live that long, it was quite natural that many people should have half believed that there was basis for the charge that I was too feeble to perform public service. To those that knew me or had seen me the absurdity of the charge was obvious. I was then and am still actively in charge of my business affairs and employ approximately four thousand men. Shortness of memory has been the least of my failings. I recall vividly, as this record of events will probably show, incidents that occurred three-quarters of a century ago; and my capacity for keeping in mind dates and places has astonished my friends.

That my seventy-nine years did not weigh heavily upon me must have been observed by those who saw me; for everywhere I stopped in the seven counties I visited, the majority I polled was appreciably larger than elsewhere. When the final test came I won by a plurality of 10,000 votes, carried thirty-nine out of seventy-one counties and was second in twenty. Had I been able to visit all of the counties I could, I am convinced, have brought the plurality up to between sixty and seventy-five thousand.

It seemed that the gravest of my difficulties were over, but I soon realized that they had just begun. Despite the primary law, which had been one of the conspicuous reforms the La Follette wing of the party had demanded and to the enactment of which I had contributed much, my election was by no means assured. When it came to carrying out the purposes of the measure the legislature cast it lightly aside and I was made to pay the penalty on grounds that were afterward proven to be fictitious.

The legislature met and the La Follette members of the Senate declared against me. With them four Democrats and one Socialist joined forces, giving them a majority in the upper house. The Assembly was in my favor. On January 26, the two houses met separately. The Senate I carried by one vote and the Assembly by an ample majority. Even after this I was not to be permitted to receive my commission without a prolonged struggle. The next day the two houses held a joint session, and all that was necessary under the law was the reading of the journals and the formal announcement of my election. This was prevented by the Lieutenant-Governor, John Strange, a La Follette supporter, who refused to put the question.

In the meantime my own supporters grew lax in their efforts and when the joint session convened each day thereafter I fell short of the number of votes necessary to elect. Sometimes, however, I missed by a very narrow margin. On one occasion I lacked but one vote. C. E. Estabrook, of Milwaukee, a member of the Assembly, who professed to be my friend, voted for Edmunds, my campaign manager.

Had he voted for me the contest would have been closed. As it was the struggle went on until March 4, when I was finally elected by a majority of three votes.

The La Follette Republicans, however, left no stone unturned to encompass my defeat. Meanwhile a joint committee of the legislature was appointed to investigate the primary election, the Senate members of which were Messrs. Marsh and Morris — two La Follette Republicans — and Husting, a Democrat from Dodge County, who has since been elected to the United States Senate, all of whom were opposed to me. Five members were appointed by the Assembly.

The proceedings of that investigation have become a part of public record. To repeat the history of the long and dreary undertaking would be superfluous here. Every check that I paid out — representing in the aggregate $107,000 — was submitted for examination. Every item of expense was accounted for so far as the brief time at our disposal during the campaign permitted. The experience was a costly and disagreeable one for me. My secretary and many other persons were summoned as witnesses and told in detail what had been done. My bank accounts and books were scrutinized as evidence. Everything that could possibly afford information was laid bare. As a result of the inquiry my added expenses were in excess of $20,000.

The whole proceeding, which was instituted in large part by J. J. Blaine, one of the most radical La Follette followers, to whom I had given $1,000 some years before, was summed up by the investigating committee in its majority report as follows:

Political, partisan, or other charges may always be preferred in the legislature against any man nominated, and used as an excuse to defeat the will of the people as expressed at the primary. Personal, factional, and political reasons were responsible

in most instances for the attempt to repudiate the primary during
the last session of the legislature. Almost every subterfuge and
excuse imaginable was resorted to by some Republicans even to
the extent of caucusing with Democrats and Social Democrats,
to defeat the Republican party nominee. Members were coerced
to absent themselves from the sessions day after day to prevent a
quorum being present. Members were flattered and cajoled by
complimentary votes to defeat an election. Caucuses were held
when the purpose of the law was to avoid caucusing. Specific
charges were preferred to supply an excuse for defeating the
people's expressed wish, and yet a subsequent investigation of
these charges showed that Senator Blaine who preferred them
"never pretended to have enough evidence to convict any candidate in the primary" and only preferred them "to set this
thing in motion," according to his own testimony. This investigation was urged by many for factional and political purposes
only, and to defeat the Republican party nominee. The large
expenditure of money by Republican candidates was known to the
electorate at the time of the primary nomination as well as it was
known to the members of the legislature later.

Here I might moralize at some length, if I were so
minded, upon the rectitude of political maneuvering. The
expenditure of money seems to be a relative thing, the
moral turpitude depending upon not how but for what it is
spent. For all of the money I devoted to the upbuilding and
promotion of the Half-breed faction, the election of La
Follette as Governor, and the smashing of the old inner
ring of the Republican party, in direct campaign contributions and donations to candidates and for the establishment of a newspaper to give voice to the cause, the great
cause of which, I had been told, I was "the source of unfail-
ing power," I was commended in terms so flattering that
I hesitate to set them down here. For spending one-
fifth of that amount upon my own election under the most
adverse circumstances and in the face of the most bitter

and unscrupulous opposition, I was condemned out of hand. The practice that was justified in the one case was condemned as most reprehensible in the other. The primary election put forward as one of the cardinal principles of progressive reform was tossed aside without even the good grace of an explanation.

The expenditures of some of the other candidates were by no means small and time was when an outlay for a senatorial campaign far greater than mine had not evoked denunciation. More than once during this period I was reminded of the election of John L. Mitchel, whom I knew very well, in whose behalf, I have heard it said on good authority, $250,000 was expended. General Bragg, the defeated candidate, also my friend, observed that he had been shot with a gold bullet. None the less Mitchel escaped indictment for political manslaughter.

The men who took the most conspicuous part in the fight against me in Wisconsin were the political associates of La Follette. The whole trend of affairs indicated that the opposition was well organized, and certainly it was most persistent. Senator Sanborn, of Ashland, a La Follette Republican, met me in the Pfister Hotel in Milwaukee shortly after the primary election and said, as he shook hands with me, that I had won fairly and that he would support me. Subsequently in an interview he made the same statement. When he entered the legislature, however, the existence of a primary law and his apparent convictions availed nothing. Whether he changed his mind or acted in accordance with orders from higher up, he voted against me. This and other incidents indicated how persevering the opposition was.

Vindication in the state legislature did not bring my troubles to an end. My opponents in the state Senate, failing in their first move, clung tenaciously to their purpose and carried the fight up to the United States Senate, where a small group of progressive Republicans, at that time more or less cohesive, took the initiative in demanding an investigation. Here the controversy bore a slightly different aspect. The agitation over campaign expenditures was on. The so-called progressive ideas were expanding and my election served as a convenient peg upon which to hang declarations of political probity for the delectation of the voters to whom the progressive appeal was addressed. Here again no specific charges were brought forward; the violation of no law was alleged. Had it not been for the hue and cry raised over the progressive propaganda, I am convinced that the Senate would never have taken the trouble to make the investigation.

But the time was for me unpropitious. The whole story was gone over a second time. Witnesses were summoned again; every detail of the campaign was scrutinized by the Senate investigating committee. Two large volumes of testimony attest the energy of the investigators. When the inquiry was concluded a report was brought in upholding the validity of my election. After a period of protracted debate covering a wide range of subjects, not a few of which had little to do with the law or morals of campaign expenditures, the report was adopted by the Senate. Fortunately there were men of conviction in that body and my vindication I owe to them.

At last the fight was over and I was secure in my position. But the bitter experience had cost me many an illusion — perhaps the greatest loss I had sustained — and shook my faith in human kind.

For almost seventy years I had dealt with all sorts and conditions of men. I had blazed trails with them through the forest, spread my blanket beside theirs on the snow, logged with them in the winter camps, and shared with them the dangers of log driving and sailing vessels on the lakes. Thousands I have taught the way of lumbering. In my employ I have had and now have grandfather, father, and son working together. I have also known men of large affairs — merchants, railroad builders, manufacturers, capitalists — to whose energy and foresight the developed country is a monument. None of these has suffered loss through me.

It remained for me in these later days to discover how quickly, in the come and go of politics, convictions can be discarded, principles abandoned, and obligations overlooked, and how readily the gauge of political progress veers to the currents of political animosity and ambition.

To sum up, I had laid the plans and given the impetus which resulted in the organization of the Half-breed faction, to which was due the sanely progressive legislation enacted in Wisconsin. I had contributed to the campaign funds of La Follette and many of his lieutenants, most of whom, I believe, would never have held political office if left to their own resources. In the aggregate I had expended approximately $500,000. For this I had been assured that without me the history of this achievement would have been a blank page.

The moral of this narrative I leave for others to draw. From a large view it affords, I think, food for reflection, particularly as to the value of the primary. In setting out to correct abuses by this method, is it not possible that we have opened the way for other abuses? By the limitation of campaign expenditures for legitimate purposes,— arousing popular interest in problems of government and putting before the electorate the political issues involved in an election,— has not the political system been modified to the advantage of the party or faction in control of the machinery of government and of party organization, giving them an advantage almost impossible to overcome? Do the people really take sufficient interest in primaries to make them gauges of the actual trend of popular thought? These are perplexing questions and I shall not attempt to answer them, but I believe that in time they will demand a reply.

My work in the political field is done. Upon the expiration of my last term in the Senate it was with relief that I announced that I would no longer seek public office, although even then many had urged me to keep on. I was quite willing to leave that to younger men who rightly aspire to political place.

CHAPTER XXI

Social phenomena of past three-quarters of a century — Adaptability of human nature — Hardships of old made for contentment — Inventions and luxuries of recent development and extravagant tastes of modern period — Development of professions and excess of professional men — Experiences in medicine — Lawyers and litigation — Sleep and efficiency — Accuracy of present narrative.

CASTING back over my experiences of almost fourscore years in this cursory fashion brings into rather strong relief, in my own mind at least, some interesting social phenomena which have been lost sight of under the shadow of more important and more conspicuous events.

The readiness with which human beings adapt themselves to their environment and the conditions of living oftentimes outranges the comprehensibility of those whose experiences are embraced within a limited field and an unvaried manner of living. Within my own lifetime the changes have been vast. It is difficult sometimes to convince people of the present day that human nature was able to withstand the rigors we repeatedly encountered three-quarters of a century ago, and the recital of some of my own experiences will probably be received with some incredulity. The whole fabric of living has been altered within that time. The things that go to make up the day's routine, work or play, are different. And who knows what changes the next fifty years will have wrought?

Nevertheless, human nature has conformed to the changes that have occurred with much greater facility than might

be imagined by those whose span of life has been too short
to enable them to realize their extent. People met with
equanimity the rigors of old. With probably too much
equanimity they have accepted the comforts and luxuries
of the new scale of living, a fact worthy of consideration
in weighing the morals of our present community life.

In my early boyhood in New Brunswick, one of the
oldest settled regions on the western continent, work began
at early dawn, as I have said, and continued until darkness brought it to an end. Every family was clothed with
the wool from its own flock of sheep grazed on the commons, and the carding, spinning, weaving, and knitting
went on incessantly. There were no stoves nor lamps nor
many of the conveniences now regarded as necessities.
Domestic activity centered upon the big open hearths, and
for artificial light we depended upon candles of our own
molding. No moment was wasted. The exigencies of
the time afforded no leisure. And even these conditions,
I have no doubt, were an improvement upon those which
confronted the greater number of immigrants to the western
world.

Yet life seemed to hold its full measure of happiness.
There was no idleness to breed discontent. There were no
false standards of living to stir up dissatisfaction and
envy. The luxuries which now afford so many opportunities for excursions into the field of extravagance simply
did not exist.

In the isolated logging camps in New Brunswick, Maine,
Michigan, and Wisconsin, almost completely cut off from
the world at large by the formidable winters, the same
routine prevailed. The limited fare of salt pork, beans,
bread, tea, and molasses was unvarying. Yet men thrived
upon it and were reasonably content. Nor did they suffer

for lack of more diversified sustenance. From this point of view their health was better than that of workmen of the present day.

Even greater contrasts are reached by comparison of modern conditions with those which confronted the voyageurs, the timber explorers, in which capacity I traversed many miles of territory bordering upon Green Bay and the upper lakes. Sometimes when the snow lay deep in the forest and the temperature reached thirty and thirty-five degrees below zero, we slept in the open without a fire and only a pair of blankets to cover us. Nor did we have cooked food,— only what we were able to carry in our knapsacks fortified by a cup of hot tea. In the summer-time conditions were almost as uncomfortable. The rains beat down upon us, for we were without shelter of any kind, and in forcing our way through the thick underbrush our clothes were saturated. Yet we were none the worse for these experiences, nor did we suffer from the afflictions supposed nowadays to result from them.

Many of the conveniences for which our latter-day civilization is conspicuous were unknown three-quarters of a century ago. Railroads were just beginning to be built. The telephone, electric lights, and a hundred other inventions had not yet been evolved. But all of these, while answering to our needs, have at the same time provided opportunity for extravagance, the national weakness of the American people. No sooner does the automobile make its appearance, by way of illustration, than it becomes an obsession and people that can ill afford to buy them are put to extraordinary extremities to emulate those who are able to maintain one. Improvement of railroads has stimulated the passion for travel and on every side newly discovered luxuries rapidly come to be regarded as necessities, and dissatisfaction and discontent follow in the wake of overindulgence.

There is now much talk of the high cost of living. If we lived as we did a half-century or more ago, our expenditures for necessities would be a third less than then. But it is not the necessities that are absorbing the incomes of to-day. It is the rapid advance in the scale of living, the demand for more conveniences, for greater luxury, and the insatiable appetite of human nature for novelty. The essentials of progress, labor, and thrift are too often lost sight of in the rush to adopt new facilities which are of value as aids to industry but detrimental when made the ends to be attained.

Because of the rather unusual position I occupied in the logging camps and lumber settlements and my opportunities for observation, it is but natural that I should be struck by the more recent phenomena that have appeared with the advent of doctors and the multiplication of drug stores. In our isolated camps sickness was rare. Most of the minor and many of the major ills we seemed to escape. I do not wish to disparage the work of physicians. I have known many excellent ones. Among them was Dr. Hall, one of the pioneer lumbermen of the Menominee River. Despite the primitive conditions under which we lived, he never lost a case of typhoid, a common disease in the early days along the river, if he gave it careful attention. I remember one occasion when there were eleven mill employees in Menominee in one room, all afflicted with it, some of whose tongues were parched and cracked with the fever. All of them under Dr. Hall's ministrations recovered as expeditiously, perhaps, as they would have had we enjoyed the facilities of a modern hospital.

With the flood of doctors poured out upon the country after a perfunctory university education I have little patience. We succeeded in getting on very well without them. None the less, human nature, with the same facility with which it adapted itself to the old order, has embraced the new and has developed all manner of ills calling for the attention of physicians and the absorption of drugs and medicines.

Some diseases have even made their appearance as fads which have been assiduously cultivated by the doctors who profited by them. A number of years ago, for example, the country appeared to be in the throes of appendicitis, and many misguided persons partook of grapes and other fruits in fear and trembling lest they swallowed a seed which might lodge in the vermiform appendix. I myself appealed to Dr. Isham, at one time dean of the medical profession in Chicago, who happened to be taking breakfast at my house. "There is not much appendicitis," he said. "There never was. I eat grapes, seeds and all." Then came the scientific revelation that a seed had never been discovered in the appendix, the opening of which is too small to permit one to lodge there.

In spite of this, thousands of persons were subjected to operations, some of whom died; and the fear was so general that one woman I knew informed me that she was going to the hospital for another ailment and purposed to have her appendix cut out at the same time to avoid the possibility of having the disease. That particular fad has passed, but others have succeeded it and the innumerable doctors always find a way of keeping occupied.

The quantity of medicines consumed has gone on increasing at a rapid rate, for no apparent reason. Early experiences and close observation have led me to the conclusion that nature will work its own curative effects and that the elaborate formulæ devised by physicians oftentimes becloud the ailment, to the dismay of the patient but to the advantage of the druggist as well as the doctor. The drugs upon which I have come to rely are meager. When the "ague-and-chill fever" prevailed in the Middle West, and I as well as everybody else suffered with it, I came to appreciate the value of quinine. It was used sparingly for many years and administered only with fourth-proof brandy; but I took liberal doses, sometimes a spoonful, and suffered no ill effects. For many years I had been subject to very pronounced attacks of influenza. The quinine, which appeared to be stimulating in its effects, prevented these, I discovered, if taken when the symptoms first became manifest. I also found that snuff did much to relieve the congestion in the nasal passages. For me, at least, these two remedies have been of incalculable value, and for the past nine years I have never been afflicted with a "cold." Although repeatedly threatened with them I have warded them off so successfully that I can defy them with confidence. Another medicine which I have used for forty years, at the suggestion of Dr. Isham, to keep the digestive tract clear is aloes. These have been for me, at least, sufficient to ward off ordinary ills and my continued good health I owe in large measure to them.

The objection that may be taken to the multiplication of doctors may be applied with equal force to lawyers, judging by the perspective of seventy years. They, of course, have their place in the scheme of civilization as well as physicians, but in the early settlements along Green Bay we did very well without them. Now the universities turn them out by the thousands every year and every community is overcrowded with them. Instead of simplifying life their activities have complicated it, and litigation over trivial things clogs the courts and has become a positive evil, especially in the United States. The assertion has been made that there is more litigation in Cook County, Illinois, than in England, and I am inclined to believe that it is true.

I have so tried to regulate my own affairs as to avoid lawsuits or legal entanglements and have succeeded, I think, very well. I have never had a personal lawsuit, never gave my note and endorsed only one, never borrowed a dollar. The suits entered against the companies of which I have had charge have been very few and unimportant. I have managed the affairs of the N. Ludington Company at Marinette, which has done an extensive business, for more than fifty-seven years. For the first fifty years of this time less than fifty dollars was paid in legal fees nor was it involved in a lawsuit. All deeds, of which there were thousands, were prepared in the office of the company and there was never occasion to call for legal counsel or aid.

To sum up, the extraordinary increase in the number of professional men, many of whom are social parasites, has gone on at such a pace in this country, which is becoming overcrowded with them, that it constitutes a sociological fact which must sooner or later be pondered carefully if the nation is to continue in the path of progress. Fundamentally the strength of a nation depends upon its productivity and its productivity depends primarily upon the soil — the farms, mines, and forests. Processes of production, of course, need to be studied and manufacture is essential, but the function of the so-called professions is secondary, to keep the machinery of production running smoothly and to promote the efficiency of the human race. Beyond that point they have no reason for existence and are a sociological encumbrance. Such, at least, is the moral to be drawn from a comparison of present-day conditions with those which prevailed when the Middle West was in the awakening.

Two or three generations ago a far larger proportion of the day was given up to labor than at present. I am not sure that there was even less time for sleep. My own habits in this respect are probably somewhat exceptional and I mention them only because of the general interest in the subject. Mr. Ogden, as I have said, a man of tremendous energy, worked eighteen hours out of twenty-four and seemed to require only a few hours of sleep to keep himself at the highest point of efficiency. Since my twentieth year I have found that four or five hours suffice for me. While others in the camps were asleep, I read far into the night, poring over the *Congressional Globe* and medical books or thinking over business affairs and laying plans for the future. This rule I have followed throughout my life, much to my own advantage, I have no doubt.

I could moralize at length on a hundred different facts of our present-day existence as emphasized by a comparison with our manner of living long ago; but it would be, I fear, to no purpose, as the world is made and we cannot change it. Likewise my reminiscences might be expanded to fill volumes. What I have written here is but a bare outline. Such as it is, however, it will be found to be accurate. My memory has always served me well, and in casting back over the years it has been no task for me to recall day and date, time and place. From the period when, at the age of three, having been put to bed with the measles, I slipped out of the house and walked barefooted in the snow, much to my mother's alarm, down to the present, I recall vividly all sorts of incidents in my career. Names I do not remember so easily, probably because I have known and employed so many men that it has been impossible to keep them all in mind.

I realize that in the ever-busy present interest in the lesser affairs of the past is not keen, and it is not my purpose to overburden this record with the recital of insignificant events. I give it to the reader for what it is worth; and if, as I have said, the scrutiny of the present from the perspective of three-quarters of a century will enable anyone to judge with clearer vision, I shall count what is here written as of some value.